Called to Freedom

Called to Freedom
Liberation Theology and the Future of Christian Doctrine

Daniel L. Migliore

The Westminster Press
Philadelphia

First edition
Published by The Westminster Press ®
Philadelphia, Pennsylvania

PRINTED IN THE UNITED STATES OF AMERICA

9 8 7 6 5 4 3 2 1

Library of Congress Cataloging in Publication Data

Migliore, Daniel L   1935–
  Called to freedom.

  Includes bibliographical references.
  1. Freedom (Theology) 2. Liberation theology.
I. Title.
BT810.2.M53   261.8   79-21879
ISBN 0-664-24289-8

In Memory of My Father

Contents

Acknowledgments

I wish to express my appreciation to the President and the Board of Trustees of Princeton Theological Seminary for a sabbatical leave in the academic year 1977–78, during which this book was written. I am also grateful to my colleagues Hugh T. Kerr, Charles C. West, and George W. Stroup III, who read the manuscript at various stages and made helpful criticisms, and to my wife, Margaret, who did all the typing and gave me constant encouragement.

Introduction

The Christian story must be retold again and again in terms that are understandable to people here and now. How is this story to be told in our time? Who is Christ for us today, and how are we to understand the salvation he brings? Briefly stated, the answer to these questions that I wish to explore in the following pages is that the gospel is the good news of God's liberation of those in bondage and of his call to freedom. The Christian gospel is a message of freedom: the astonishing freedom of God for us, the gift of freedom that is ours in faith, and the responsible exercise of this new freedom. As I hope to show, this message of God's gift and call to freedom is of the greatest importance to the struggle for liberation from all forms of bondage so characteristic of our time.

That the Christian gospel and human freedom are intimately connected is hardly a discovery of recent theology. According to one Gospel account, Jesus began his ministry by proclaiming release to the captives and liberty to the oppressed (Luke 4:18). The apostle Paul understood the work of Christ and his Spirit as liberating. "For freedom Christ has set us free" (Gal. 5:1). "Where the Spirit of the Lord is, there is freedom" (II Cor. 3:17). The Protestant Reformers of the sixteenth century wrote passionately and extensively on Christian freedom. In 1934 the German Confessing Church at Barmen opposed the claims of a totalitar-

ian state by bearing witness to the sole lordship of Christ and
the freedom of his disciples to love and serve others. At
critical points in its history, the church has become more
fully aware of the integral relationship between the redemptive activity of God and the rise of a new human freedom.

Today the church faces the challenge to extend still further its understanding of the bond between the gospel and the
liberation of the oppressed. This challenge is called the "theology of liberation," and it comes primarily from Christians
in the third world, black Christians, and Christian women.
Despite real limitations, this theological development is by
far the most creative and penetrating of the last decade.
While there are many differences among the representatives
of this theology, they are agreed that salvation includes the
struggle for liberation. God's creative and redemptive activity is the ultimate basis and fulfillment of the process by
which people break free from all forms of enslavement.
Human beings are in bondage not only to their own sinfulness but also to economic, social, and political powers of this
world. God wills all people to be free and to live in an
inclusive community characterized by justice and friendship
instead of exploitation and hostility.

In the five chapters that make up this little book, I wish
to affirm *both the importance and the limits* of interpreting
the gospel today as God's liberating activity in which we
are called to take part. The method I have chosen is to
rethink five basic Christian doctrines in the light of the liberation theme. I do not claim that these chapters constitute
a comprehensive, systematic theology of freedom, although
I hope they may be helpful steps in that direction. Nor do
I pretend to speak as one who has personally experienced
the oppression of the poor of the third world or of blacks
and other minority groups in the United States. My own
social context as a Christian theologian is the predomi-
nantly middle-class church in North America. In these
pages I wish to address primarily the members of this
church, for the need to experience, celebrate, and practice

the gospel of liberation is nowhere greater than here. As a seminary teacher responsible for helping to prepare young men and women for Christian ministry, I know firsthand how urgent and yet how precarious a task it is to connect the freedom announced by the gospel both to the struggles of oppressed peoples and to the different but nonetheless real conditions of bondage of more affluent individuals and nations. Often we deeply resist this effort, not least because of our privatistic and otherworldly understandings of the Bible and of basic Christian doctrines.

Several convictions inform the following chapters, and it is well for me to state these at the outset. The first conviction is that *the effort to rethink Christian faith and practice in terms of the process of liberation is not a passing fad but a necessary task of the church.* The necessity arises both out of the social situation of the Christian church today and out of the Christian gospel itself. At least since the Enlightenment, the history of humanity has been increasingly understood as a history of the struggle for freedom. During this same period, the teachings and practices of the church have been under growing, and all too often justified, attack as being opponents of freedom and predictable allies of the established order of things, whatever that happens to be. If Christian faith is to be presented in a compelling way to people today, it will have to be made clear that the God of the gospel does not compete with genuine human freedom but is its ultimate author and advocate. The way we read the Bible and the way we understand the basic doctrines of Christian faith will have to express unmistakably that Christianity is "the religion of an exceedingly great freedom."[1] We are a long way from that goal in the churches of North America.

A second conviction is that *the attempt to reformulate the faith in the language of freedom and to reorder the mission of the church toward the practice of freedom must be a critical undertaking.* "Liberation" and "freedom" are ambiguous words. They are often employed today as easy slogans by both conservatives and radicals. However, we are not left

with the unhappy alternative of either becoming sloganeers
or simply avoiding the language of freedom altogether in our
interpretation of the Christian message for our time. All
words can be misused or cheapened; all have ambiguous
histories and carry heavy burdens. There are no pure, innocent words which in themselves are perfectly suited to convey
God's good news. That was true in New Testament times and
it is true today. Nevertheless, there are more or less appropriate words to communicate what the gospel is all about, and
there are more or less adequate understandings of God and
of God's relationship to the world. Whatever the hazards, I
am convinced that in our time the Christian message is most
appropriately understood as the new freedom which is both
a gift of God and a human task.

The specifically Christian meaning of freedom must be
established in a continuous and critical dialogue between the
biblical witness to the freedom of God and the understandings of freedom in modern culture. For many people in Western societies, freedom means essentially being able to do as
you please, and in particular, being free to possess and consume things limitlessly. The Christian understanding of freedom, rooted in the freedom of God made known in Jesus
Christ, is altogether different. The central thesis of this book
is that the freedom of God is not sheer arbitrariness; it is
preeminently the freedom to love. In like manner, the perfection of human freedom is to be seen not in the total absence
of limitations but in openness to and solidarity with others,
and especially with the poor, the despised, and the oppressed.
If the words "freedom" and "liberation" are admittedly
scarred by political terrorists on the one hand and by the
apologists of self-centered freedom in a consumer society on
the other, the cross of Jesus is the abiding reminder that
God's freedom is wholly other. The apostle Paul boldly proclaimed the new freedom in Christ, even if he found it necessary to distinguish this freedom from both libertinism and
legalism: "For freedom Christ has set us free. . . . You were
called to freedom . . . only do not use your freedom as an

opportunity for the flesh, but through love be servants of one another" (Gal. 5:1, 13).

Another conviction underlying this book is that *it is important for all Christians, and not simply for professional theologians like myself, to participate in the making of a theology of freedom.* Hence the chapters of this book are not technical theological studies. I have aimed to offer assistance to reflective Christians who are ready to explore the meaning of the biblical message and the doctrines of the church in relation to the cry for freedom that arises from exploited and oppressed peoples today. The future of the church depends less on the production of academic theological treatises about freedom than on the increased participation of Christian pastors and lay people in the process of relating the gospel of freedom to the various forms of human bondage evident both inside and outside the church.

A final conviction is that *the reinterpretation of Christian doctrine, however necessary, is insufficient; a deeper understanding of the faith is for the sake of more responsible Christian witness and life.* Gustavo Gutiérrez, one of the most influential theologians of liberation, rightly reminds us that "all the political theologies, the theologies of hope, of revolution and of liberation, are not worth one act of genuine solidarity with exploited social classes."[2] This is obviously not to say that theological reflection is unimportant; it is simply to say that such reflection is not an end in itself. A theology of Christian freedom must not be mere theory; it must be a new understanding of freedom that informs Christian life and practice.

By way of orientation, I will indicate briefly how the following chapters are related to my overall theme and to each other. My contention in Chapter 1 is that the church must learn to listen anew to the witness of Scripture. Do our doctrines of Scripture and our theories of interpretation allow Scripture to address us freely or do they determine in advance what Scripture must say? I maintain that the authority of Scripture lies in its message of God's liberating activity.

This message must not be narrowed in a privatistic way nor distorted to fit a comforting ideology. We should approach Scripture in genuine openness to its judging and liberating word.

Since it is not Scripture itself but the living Jesus Christ attested by Scripture who stands at the center of Christian faith and life, I ask in Chapter 2: Has Christian doctrine paid sufficient attention to the liberating activity of Jesus, to his communication of the free grace of God to the poor and the outcast? How does the gospel narrative deepen our understanding of human bondage and full liberation? What are the implications of confessing Jesus as liberator for Christian discipleship and the mission of the church today?

Chapter 3 takes up the question of how the different freedom of Jesus transforms our understanding of the freedom and power of God. The gospel of the crucified and risen Jesus revolutionizes our understanding of God and hence of what it means to be truly free as a creature in the image of God. The question of authentic human freedom is ultimately inseparable from the question of the nature of God. How then shall we interpret the distinctively Christian confession of God as triune? What light does the doctrine of the Trinity shed on the human struggle for freedom and new community?

Because our understanding of God and our understanding of ourselves go hand in hand, I focus in Chapter 4 on the doctrine of the Christian life or Christian spirituality. Does concern for the new life in Christ, for the sanctification of life through prayer, meditation, spiritual discipline, and worship conflict with active participation in the cause of liberation in the social, political, and economic spheres? Must we choose between spirituality and liberation? All too many members of the church think they must answer these questions in the affirmative. This shows how pressing the need is for the development of a new spirituality of liberation.

Finally, in Chapter 5 attention is given to the relationship between the process of liberation and different kinds of hope in face of death. I concede the truth of the charge that Christian doctrines of life after death have sometimes promoted an otherworldliness that undercuts commitment to the cause of justice and freedom in this world. But I argue that the prevailing images of death in modern American culture must also be subjected to critical examination, for they reflect a real bondage to the power of death. Properly understood, Christian hope in God who raised the crucified Jesus, far from alienating us from the struggles of the oppressed, liberates us for a life of self-expending love.

It is my hope that this book will stimulate readers to raise new questions. The freedom of Jesus is provocative and unsettling. Those who follow him are compelled to ask again and again whether they rightly understand what it means to be free as God is free.

Called to Freedom

Chapter I

Scripture as
Liberating Word

Implicitly or explicitly every Christian theology acknowledges the importance of Scripture. While reason, tradition, experience, culture, social analysis, and other factors also play a necessary role in creative theological reflection, the decisive factor must be the biblical witness. Hence we begin our study of the theological basis of human liberation by defining the authority and proper use of Scripture.

For the Protestant Reformers, the authority of Scripture was rooted in the liberating power of its message. When they acknowledged Scripture as authoritative for Christian faith and life, they were not submitting to a despotic and arbitrary power. Their appeal to "Scripture alone" was an appeal to "Christ alone." Scripture had a center: the good news of God's gracious acceptance of sinners revealed in Jesus Christ. This message authored joyful faith and established Christian freedom.

While the affirmations of scriptural authority and of new freedom in Christ were held together by the Reformers, they have fallen apart in the church today. On the one hand, the doctrine of the inerrancy of Scripture distracts the church. The central scriptural witness to God's liberating activity is missed. Scripture is read as a repository of revealed truths which must simply be accepted and obeyed. If in previous centuries passages of Scripture could be cited to defend the institution of slavery, today Scripture can be used to fight the movement of women toward new freedom in the church and in society. If in Nazi Germany many Christians could support their loyalty to the state with scriptural arguments, today Scripture can be cited against the efforts of the poor and the oppressed to throw off their bondage.

On the other hand, Scripture is authoritative for some Christian liberationists only insofar as it justifies and promotes a particular political program or movement. According to this view, Scripture possesses authority primarily as a weapon against the oppressors. Scripture helps to empower the powerless so that they may seize power from the powerful. In this reading of Scripture, the meaning of liberation is in danger of being defined by prevailing cultural norms rather than by the witness of Scripture itself.

Clearly, there is a great deal of controversy today about the authority of Scripture and about the relation of its message to the struggles for freedom in the world. The church and theology cannot escape the question: What shall we do with the Bible?[3] The answer I shall propose is: Recover its message of God's different liberating activity. Learn to hear anew its invitation to participate in the awesome freedom of God. This process of rediscovery and relearning will require radical change in our conventional ideas about Scripture.

I

The three most influential approaches to Scripture in modern Christianity have been biblicism, historicism, and privatism. Each of these approaches obscures the liberating word of Scripture. In different ways each makes Scripture a captive of a prevailing trend of culture rather than an instrument of God's Spirit of freedom.

1. The way of biblicism arose out of the church's efforts to defend the witness of Scripture against attacks on its authority. Enlightenment, secularization, and the new empha-

sis on human autonomy in the modern era challenged all traditional authority. Anxious to protect the insights of the Reformation, Protestant theologians became increasingly defensive and strident in their claims about the supernatural character of Scripture. Every book, every chapter, every verse, every word was directly inspired by God.[4] The doctrine of inspiration became a theory of the supernatural origin of Scripture. Various ideas about how this took place were advanced, including the proposal that God dictated the words of Scripture to the biblical writers, who acted as secretaries. All of these theories of inspiration held two points in common.

First, inspiration meant inspiredness. It referred to an inherent quality or property of Scripture resulting from its supernatural origin. The effect of this doctrine of inspiration was to focus attention on the alleged miraculous origin of the Bible rather than on its central message. It also encouraged the idea that Scripture was a closed system of inspired statements. With the advance of the modern historical consciousness, this view of the unity of Scripture collapsed.

Second, inspiration meant infallibility. Since God was the author of Scripture, it was without error. Charles Hodge, Princeton Seminary theologian of the mid-nineteenth century, taught that the Bible was "free from all error whether of doctrine, fact or precept."[5] This inerrancy theory was further refined by Benjamin Warfield, another Princeton theologian. Warfield argued that inerrancy was a property possessed by the original biblical autographs even if a few minor errors may have been introduced in the course of the transmission of the text. Thus, to the Roman Catholic dogma of the infallibility of the pope (1870), directed against the rising tide of modernity, there corresponded the Protestant doctrine of the infallibility of the Bible. The true basis of Christian confidence was obscured. The church wanted an absolute guarantee of its faith and proclamation; it found this guarantee in the parallel doctrines of biblical and papal infallibility. But a church with an infallible teaching office or an infallible Bible no longer allows Scripture to work as liberating word in its own way.

2. With the rise of the modern historical consciousness, a new approach to Scripture was introduced. The Bible was read simply as a historical source. What was authoritative was not the text in its received form but the "facts" behind the text as reconstructed by the historian. The contributions of the historical approach were considerable. The writings of the Bible were understood in their own historical context. The closed theological systems characteristic of both Catholic and Protestant scholasticism were shattered. Yet while helping to break the chains of scholasticism and dogmatism, the historical method created in turn a new form of the captivity of Scripture. The interest of the historian focused primarily on establishing "what really happened," what could be declared "factual." This inevitably led to what Hans Frei has called "the eclipse of biblical narrative."[6] The meaning of the Bible was separated from its literary form and located in the "facts" behind the text. These facts were then set within a new interpretative framework provided by the biblical scholar. The historicist approach allowed the Bible to speak only within the limits of the conceptualization and systematization of reality brought by the interpreter to the texts.

3. Still another approach to Scripture that appeared in modern Christianity was privatism. The authority of Scripture was located in the saving meaning which the text had for the individual. There was, of course, a legitimate concern that prompted this emphasis. Against both the speculations of scholastic theology and the obsession with past facts in modern historicism, pietism concentrated on the meaning of the Bible for the individual's salvation. The Bible speaks to me and assures me of God's forgiveness and mercy in Jesus Christ. What is significant to faith is not the crucifixion of Jesus as a bare historical fact but the message that Christ died for me. There is truth in this emphasis on the "for me" of the scriptural witness, but it is distorted when it is separated from

the meaning of Scripture "for us" and "for the world." A reduction of Scripture occurs when it serves only to illumine the history of the individual pilgrim of faith. John Bunyan's classic, *The Pilgrim's Progress,* captures only one aspect of the biblical story; for many Christians, however, it has become the whole story. In this individualistic approach, another kind of erosion of the biblical narrative occurs. The social and political realms of human life are no longer encompassed by the scriptural witness. Existentialist biblical interpretation in the twentieth century has offered a variation of this privatistic tradition. The authority of Scripture is located not in its supernatural origin nor in its report of past facts but in its direct summons of the individual to new self-understanding. This individualistic interpretation of Scripture represents a retreat of the church and theology. The public realm is abandoned in favor of the private realm of life where faith can be secure from attack.

These all-too-familiar approaches to Scripture are still with us. They are restrictive and confining. Until we get beyond them, the gospel of liberation of all who are in bondage will continue to escape us.

II

Beyond the dead letter of biblicism, the unselfcritical assumptions of historicism, and the narrowness of bourgeois privatism lies the message of Scripture. It is a mysterious and scandalous message. As Karl Barth contended, "Within the Bible there is a strange, new world, the world of God."[7]

For Barth as for the Reformers, the "strange, new world" of God within the Bible has its center in the history of Jesus Christ. Long before Barth, Luther had pursued a Christ-centered interpretation of Scripture with astonishing boldness. "The well-known criterion of Luther was to test every Scripture by whether 'it sets forth Christ or not.' 'What teacheth not Christ is not apostolic, even though Peter or

Paul teacheth it. Again what preacheth Christ is apostolic, even though Judas, Annas, Pilate and Herod doth it.' "[8] This is a daring doctrine of the authority of Scripture. Not everything Scripture happens to say is authoritative. What carries authority is the proclamation of God's liberating grace in Jesus Christ.

According to Barth, Scripture is the Word of God in a derivative sense. Scripture is witness to the living Word of God decisively present in Jesus Christ. Because it functions as the unique and irreplaceable witness to Christ, Scripture is acknowledged by the church to be the norm of its faith and life.

God decisively addresses us in a human being, Jesus of Nazareth. That "the Word became flesh" (John 1:14) means that the Word of God was expressed in a concrete human life, not deposited in a collection of writings. The Bible witnesses to God's presence in the history of a particular people and decisively in the life, death, and resurrection of Jesus. As witness, the Bible does not call attention to itself. "A real witness," Barth insisted, "is not identical with that to which it witnesses, but it sets it before us."[9] An authentic witness directs our awareness to some other reality. Barth often described the function of a witness by referring to the Isenheim altarpiece by the painter Matthias Grünewald in which the figure of the crucified Lord is central. To one side of the cross stands John the Baptist, his abnormally long index finger pointing to the crucified. The inscription reads: "He must increase, but I must decrease."

While historically and culturally conditioned, the witness of the Bible by the power of the Holy Spirit becomes again and again God's word to us. The Spirit of God uses the polyphonic witness of the biblical writers to confront us with the strange, new world of God. There is no such thing as Bibleless Christianity.

The Bible is a witness, and it attests Christ. These are necessary elements of a right understanding of Scripture. But they are not sufficient. As Barth never tired of emphasizing,

the witness of Scripture is strange and new not simply because it points to Christ but because it points to the crucified
Christ; not simply because it praises the eternally rich God
but because it proclaims that this God became one of the
poor; not simply because it speaks of God's judgment and
grace but because it declares that God stands on the side of
the poor and the oppressed and judges the exalted and the
powerful. This is the revolutionary message of the Bible, and
in it is contained the seed of the whole history of human
liberation.

For Barth the history attested in Scripture is the beginning
of a new world, a new heaven and a new earth, new relationships, new community, new politics. The activity of God is
world-transforming. Of course, the strange, new world of
God includes personal transformation. The liberation of the
individual from the egocentrism, isolation, apathy, and hopelessness of existence in bondage to sin and death is of fundamental importance. Nevertheless, the history of liberation
attested in Scripture cannot be limited to the individual nor
to a private zone of life. It reaches out to all people and to
the whole creation. Scripture witnesses to the "great history
of liberation" within which the history of the liberation of the
individual has its proper and necessary place.[10]

The political meaning of Barth's radically evangelical interpretation of Scripture became evident above all in the
German church struggle during the Third Reich. It was all
too easy for some Protestants to combine their Christian faith
with Nazi ideology by noting that obedience to those in
power was enjoined by Scripture. Over against this corrup-
tion of the Scripture principle, Barth and other leaders of the
German Confessing Church declared at Barmen in 1934:
"Jesus Christ . . . is the one Word of God which we have to
hear . . . and obey in life and in death." Resistance to Hitler
on the part of these confessing Christians was a direct consequence of their rediscovery of the gospel in Scripture, the
good news of God's freedom for us in Jesus Christ and of the
new human freedom which we have in him.

III

In the later volumes of the *Church Dogmatics,* Barth interpreted the saving activity of God in Jesus Christ as a history
of reconciliation. One of his key biblical texts was II Cor.
5:19: "In Christ God was reconciling the world to himself."
This theme of God's reconciliation of sinful humanity in
Jesus Christ was developed with great imaginative power and
depth by Barth and provided the focus of his interpretation
of Scripture.

Obviously influenced by Barth's emphasis, the Confession
of 1967 of the United Presbyterian Church employed the
theme of reconciliation as its basic principle of biblical interpretation. "God's reconciling work in Jesus Christ and the
mission of reconciliation to which he has called his church
are the heart of the gospel in any age. Our generation stands
in peculiar need of reconciliation in Christ. Accordingly this
Confession of 1967 is built upon that theme. . . . The Bible
is to be interpreted in the light of its witness to God's work
of reconciliation in Christ."[11] There is much to commend the
choice of reconciliation as the central category for the interpretation of the Bible and the proclamation of the gospel
today. The Confession of 1967 clearly has in mind not only
the alienation of people from God but also their alienation
from each other as evident in the nuclear arms race, the
plight of the poor, racism, and sexism. Our alienation from
God and from each other is overcome in Christ. The ministry
of reconciliation has both vertical and horizontal dimensions.

Despite its strengths, this focus on the theme of reconciliation has limitations. Recent theologies of liberation have
helped us to understand that if God's saving activity must be
seen as a reconciling event, it must also be seen as a history
of liberation. If reconciliation emphasizes the purpose and
goal of God's activity, liberation emphasizes the process
through which that goal is attained.

Liberation theology finds the center of Scripture in its story of God's liberating activity. In the Old Testament, God's saving action is focused in the exodus, the liberation of a people from political, cultural, and religious bondage. By this event God has become known as the liberating God. "I am the LORD your God, who brought you out of the land of Egypt, out of the house of bondage" (Ex. 20:2). In the exodus God is identified not as a metaphysical absolute nor as the savior of souls but as the liberator of a people. When Israel experienced captivity again in later centuries, the promises of the prophets were cast in the image of a second exodus (Isa. 51:9–11). This new exodus would eventuate in a comprehensive and universal liberation to include not only Israel but all peoples. Even the natural environment would be transformed (Isa. 41:17–20). Thus the Old Testament history of liberation opens out into eschatology and messianism, and it is within the horizon of this hope of comprehensive liberation that the New Testament is to be understood. For Christian faith, Jesus' forgiveness of sinners, his table fellowship with despised people, his ministry to the poor and the sick, and finally his crucifixion and resurrection, constitute an anticipatory realization of God's kingdom of freedom, justice, and peace throughout the world. The biblical story of liberation summons us not only to be the free persons we have been enabled to be through Christ but also to serve the cause of the liberation of all people in all dimensions of life.

The theme of liberation in the Bible has been articulated most powerfully by theologians speaking out of particular situations of exploitation and bondage: the poverty and deprivation of millions of people in the third world, and the economic and cultural abuse suffered by blacks, women, and other disadvantaged groups in the United States. According to liberation theology, talk of reconciliation as the central message of the Bible is too readily understood in the middle-class church as a painless and superficial process requiring no fundamental changes in the existing order of society. Authentic reconciliation, however, presupposes a costly history of liberation in which people are freed both from the attitudes and conditions of slaves and from the pretenses and fears of masters. The theology of liberation assumes that people who experience chronic negation and abuse have a sensitivity to a dimension of the biblical message that has been neglected and even repressed by Christians living in relative affluence.

The process of liberation involves conflict. At the personal level it requires a break with past attitudes, habits, and ways of life in which the self is glorified. To be liberated from the powers of sin and death is to be "converted," turned away from the self to God and our neighbors. Similarly, liberation in the social realm from the forces of racism, sexism, economic exploitation, and the rape of the environment does not happen without a struggle. Christian faith and hope do not reconcile us to structures of evil; they set us in opposition to all forms of bondage. As Jürgen Moltmann writes: "Those who hope in Christ can no longer put up with reality as it is, but begin to suffer under it, to contradict it. Peace with God means conflict with the world, for the goad of the promised future stabs inexorably into the flesh of every unfulfilled present."[12]

While focus on God's liberating activity in the interpretation of Scripture both complements and corrects the understanding of Scripture centered on God's reconciling activity, the reverse is also true. Liberation and reconciliation presuppose each other. Reconciliation presupposes liberation in execution. Liberation presupposes reconciliation in intention. The biblical understanding of God's liberating activity is characterized by this bond between liberation and reconciliation. For the Bible bears witness to God who is free for others.

The interrelation of liberation and reconciliation in the biblical witness underscores the fact that all of the conceptualities and categories employed in the interpretation of the Bible must be continually reshaped by the biblical message rather than being imposed upon it. The history of Jesus defines finally what Christians mean by the freedom of God and what it means to be truly free as a human being. Consequently, the church must remain open to Scripture. It must allow the biblical story of God's liberating activity and call to freedom to reform and transform all our provisional understandings. While the church must be bold in its efforts to discern afresh the heart of the biblical message, while the church must take the risk of defining from time to time "the canon within the canon," it must test these interpretations of Scripture again and again by new study of Scripture. When the church fails to remain open to the correction and guidance of Scripture, it becomes the captive of its own doctrinal tradition and ethos or the mere echo of the dominant movements and ideologies of contemporary culture.[13]

IV

If the content of Scripture is appropriately described today as the story of God's liberating activity, which has its focus in Jesus of Nazareth, the following principles of interpretation may be proposed.

1. Scripture must be interpreted *historically;* yet the history of liberation that it attests resists our fixation on the past. The history recounted in Scripture is open and unfinished; it will find its completion only in the universal freedom and joy of God's kingdom.

Historical study of the Bible is important for many reasons. To begin with, it makes us take seriously the particularity of God's actions. If God becomes known through events at particular times and places, then the historical study of the Bible is the way we respect the historical particularity of revelation and the coming of salvation. The people of Israel are a particular people. Jesus of Nazareth is a particular human being. The Bible proclaims the liberating acts of God by naming particular places, events, persons. Of course, historical investigation cannot prove that this or that event is an act of God, but it can clarify the particularity of the history in which faith discerns God's action.

Historical study of the Bible serves a second theologically important function. Not only does it help us to recognize the historical concreteness of revelation; it also continually reminds us that the biblical writers were limited, fallible human beings. To deny their finitude is to rob them of their humanity. God does not have to destroy the humanity of the biblical witnesses in order to work through them. The grace of God does not destroy human freedom but rather establishes it.

If we are embarrassed by the humanity of the biblical writers, we are also probably embarrassed by the humanity of Jesus the Jew from Nazareth and by our own humanity. The denial of the full humanity of Jesus is docetism, i.e., Jesus only appeared to be human. This docetic heresy also insinuates itself into some doctrines of Scripture. We are docetists if we claim that the biblical witnesses were mere automatons set in motion by the Spirit of God. We are implicitly docetists if we refuse to read the Bible historically. The docetist confuses limitation with sinfulness. Jesus was without sin, but he was nevertheless limited. He did not know everything. The love of God came to us in and through a finite, limited human life. If we affirm the full humanity of Jesus, we will also respect the humanity of the biblical witnesses.

Of course, to engage in historical study of the Bible is to accept risk. Some things which we previously held to be factual are called in question. The difference between the thought world of the Bible and our thought world widens. This is the risk of the historical study of the Bible, and it disturbs us. But the risk cannot be evaded because it is implied in the event of God's decisive self-communication in a finite human life. "The Word became flesh." The Word of God entered into the ambiguity and relativity of historical reality. The incarnation involved risk, and no doctrine of biblical authority is acceptable which denies or minimizes that risk.[14]

However, recognizing the particularity of God's liberating activity and appreciating the historical conditioning of the biblical witnesses surely do not exhaust the responsibility of the biblical interpreter. To interpret the Bible historically is to see in its narratives not only memories of past events but promises of new possibilities. Perhaps the term "story" captures better than the conventional term "history" the power of the biblical witness to expand our horizon of what is possible by the grace of God. If both Old and New Testaments have their center in narratives of God's liberating activity, these narratives were told and retold in Israel and in the early church because they were not yet finished. The biblical history of liberation is not closed but open. The gospel narratives are at once the primary form of the church's recollection of the past and a form of concrete expectation. The liberation begun in Jesus Christ points to a final liberation in which the whole creation will be set free (Rom. 8:21).

To every event belongs its future: This is a principle of all historical interpretation.[15] All the more is it a principle of the interpretation of Scripture for those who believe in the resurrection of the crucified Jesus and his living lordship. To read the Bible historically in the deepest sense is to read it with an eye to the extension of its story of God's liberating activity in Christ into our own time. We must ask of Scripture not only what past it wishes to recall but also what future it wants to open up. We should not expect the full meaning of the new freedom in Christ to have been actualized in the early church. Some of Paul's statements about the place of women in the church (e.g., I Cor. 14:34) show that he was not able to draw out all of the implications of freedom in Christ. Yet the ferment and transforming power of the story of Christ the liberator are visibly at work in the attitude of the New Testament church toward women. Episodes in the Gospels depict Jesus' new openness to and friendship with women. Paul himself composes a magna charta of freedom: "There is neither Jew nor Greek, there is neither slave nor free, there is neither male nor female; for you are all one in Christ Jesus" (Gal. 3:28). Krister Stendahl rightly describes this passage as a "breakthrough," a radical new beginning of freedom incompletely realized in the early church, yet full of promise for the future under the guidance of God's Spirit.[16] To read Scripture historically is to read it with sensitivity to the direction in which it moves and not with nostalgia for New Testament times. "For whatever was written in former days was written for our instruction, that by steadfastness and by the encouragement of the scriptures we might have hope" (Rom. 15:4).

2. Scripture must be interpreted *theocentrically;* however, the meaning of "God" is radically redefined in the biblical story of liberation.

The central actor in the biblical drama is God. Scripture witnesses to the reality of God, to the purposes of God, to the kingdom of God. The content of the biblical story is God's faithfulness in acts of judgment and mercy, in the covenant with the people of Israel and in the history of Jesus. The biblical narrative has many aspects, but in the midst of the many aspects is the central theme: the mystery of the faithful God who takes up the cause of justice, freedom, and peace on behalf of the creation oppressed by sin and misery. Scripture witnesses to the promise of God even in the midst of judgment. It declares God's benevolence toward us even in the depth of our sin: "While we were yet sinners Christ died for us" (Rom. 5:8). Scripture proclaims the decisive ratification of all God's promises in the resurrection of the crucified Jesus. "For all the promises of God find their Yes in him" (II Cor. 1:20).

Who is the God of the scriptural witness? The God of Scripture is the God who acts. God is not an abstract value or a lifeless ideal. God is creator, liberator, reconciler. God calls Abraham, Moses, and the prophets. When the people of Israel are afflicted in Egypt, God acts to deliver them. Yet God is not only the one who acts; according to the witness of Scripture, God also suffers. The liberating activity of God is defined not only in terms of the event of exodus but also in terms of the bitter pilgrimage through the wilderness.

The God of Scripture is majestic and powerful. God is great and does wonderful things (Ps. 86:10). The heavens declare the glory of God (Ps. 19:1). God is exalted in power (Job 36:22). By the power of God, Israel was liberated from bondage; by the power of God, Jesus was raised from the dead. Yet the God of Scripture exercises strange power. "Not by might, nor by power, but by my Spirit, says the LORD of hosts" (Zech. 4:6). The power of God is made known in the weakness of the cross of Jesus (I Cor. 1:18ff.).

The God of Scripture is marvelously free. God is not conditioned by any outside power. God is not hemmed in by fate. God is utterly self-determined. Yet the freedom of God according to Scripture is not sufficiently defined in this negative aspect. The freedom of God is freedom for another. God is free to take the form of a servant, to undergo humiliation and even death for the sake of others. (Phil. 2:5ff.).

Thus the biblical story of liberation does something even more basic than provoking us to a new self-understanding or providing us with a new communal identity.[17] To be sure, it does these things. But primarily the witness to God's liberating activity in Scripture newly identifies God. Who is God? What is freedom within the kingdom of God? If we are faithful to the witness of Scripture, we will not ignore these questions when we ask: Who am I? What is my freedom? Scripture revolutionizes our understanding of the power and freedom of God. The passion narrative above all calls us to new self-understanding because it first calls us to a radically new understanding of God.

A theocentric interpretation of Scripture has its focus on God whose kingdom has decisively begun in Jesus Christ but has yet to be completed. Whereas Barth tended to emphasize onesidedly the already completed history of liberation and reconciliation in Jesus Christ, the Christocentrism of Scripture is also a Christocentrism "forward."[18] The liberating history of God in Christ is anticipatory. His resurrection from the dead is the "first fruits" (I Cor. 15:23). It is the supreme ratification of God's faithfulness to the purpose of

justice and freedom, reconciliation and life for all the creation. Men and women are summoned to repentance and faith;
they are called to participate in God's liberating activity in
the world. The work of God's liberating Spirit will not be
complete until the creation is freed from all enslaving powers
and enjoys "the glorious liberty of the children of God"
(Rom. 8:21).

A theocentric interpretation of Scripture is necessarily a
political interpretation. It is political not in the sense of ad-
vancing a political program but in the sense of having to do
with the human "polis," with human life in all of its manifold
social relationships. God wills that righteousness and freedom be manifest throughout the creation.

If a theocentric interpretation of Scripture requires a continuous revolution in our understanding of God, then the
biblical story of God's liberating activity is both an authori-
zation and a continual criticism of our liberation movements.
When the church automatically reacts to liberation theology
and liberation movements with alarm, it merely demon-
strates that it no longer understands or takes seriously the
message of Scripture. At the same time, all liberation movements are exposed to powerful temptations. They are
tempted to identify God with particular groups. They are
also tempted to equate liberation with the acquisition of
power in a world where power struggles are the law of life.
The God of the biblical story, whose way of liberation is
self-giving love, is always surprisingly different from what we
imagine or wish divinity to be.

3. Scripture must be interpreted *contextually;* however,
the context of our interpretation must be increasingly open
to and inclusive of the yearnings of the whole creation to be
free.

The context of our interpretation of Scripture will always
include and will frequently begin with our own personal
awareness of captivity and yearning for freedom and new life:
with our own anxiety, guilt, frustration, alienation, loneli-
ness, and despair. In no way is this context of understanding

Scripture as liberating word to be denigrated. Unfortunately, the context of the interpretation of the biblical story of liberation for many Christians never extends beyond this essentially private realm.

The larger context for interpreting Scripture is the community of believers. The Bible is the book of the church. It is not the individual believer but the community of faith which has declared these writings to be canonical—i.e., has declared that they measure up to the rule or norm for identifying the Word of God. Thus, to interpret Scripture contextually means to listen to the biblical story in and with the community of faith, remembering that this community has heard the Word of God here before, and confidently expecting that God will again speak to us through the scriptural witness. To interpret Scripture contextually is to interpret it in the context of the memory and hope of the Christian community.

Through the centuries, that community has responded to this witness of Scripture by its faith, life, worship, and confession. We interpret Scripture contextually by allowing ourselves to be guided by the church's confessions and worship. This means being open to the wisdom and experience of the whole community of faith, which can deepen and correct our own understandings of sin and salvation, captivity and liberation. Scripture is not subordinate to the confessions and creeds of the church. They are subordinate to Scripture and are subject to reform in the light of its message. Scripture is not to be locked into the *a priori* system of a particular confessional statement. Nevertheless, the creeds and confessions are exemplary interpretations of Scripture. Rather than competing with Scripture or replacing its witness, authentic confessions declare how the central message of Scripture is to be understood in a particular moment of controversy and confusion in the church. They point with urgency to the Word of God in Scripture which is in danger of being obscured or forgotten. The church's confession of faith is not a norm to which Scripture is subjugated. It provides the

communal context in which we get our bearings for understanding Scripture afresh as witness to the activity and purposes of God manifest decisively in Jesus Christ.

But interpreting Scripture contextually, that is, in and
with the community of faith, means still more. It means we
interpret Scripture in the context of a community struggling
here and now to be receptive to God's liberating grace, obedient to God's call to freedom, in the midst of a world full of
injustice and misery. In the understanding of Scripture, reflection and practice go together. The necessary context for
interpreting Scripture is therefore practical engagement in
the living of Christian faith, love, and hope in a still un-
redeemed world. The necessary context for interpreting
Scripture is real solidarity with all oppressed people. Apart
from this context of solidarity with the poor and the despised,
every interpretation of Scripture, even if it speaks a great deal
of God's liberating activity, becomes uselessly abstract. Even
worse, it becomes a tool of our self-serving ideologies. However "objective" we may think we are, we will always interpret Scripture in some particular social context and in relation to some concrete form of life with its own interests and
presuppositions. The interpretation of Scripture is inseparable from a particular situation in life. If the theme of Scripture is the history of God's liberating activity, the interpretation of Scripture cannot be divorced from the practice of
Christian freedom. Does our interpretation of Scripture take
place in the context of a community seeking to be obedient
to the crucified and risen Lord in its concrete practice, or
does it support, reflect, and legitimize our comfortable way
of life? No proper understanding of Scripture is possible in
a context of complacency and apathy. The biblical story of
liberation will not be easily heard by those who are satisfied
with a luxurious form of life which is built on the blood of
their brothers and sisters.[19]

V

Scripture is to be interpreted historically: that is the "how" of proper interpretation. Scripture is to be interpreted theocentrically: that is the "what," the content of the witness of Scripture. Scripture is to be interpreted contextually: i.e., the struggling, engaged community of faith is the context, the "where" of the interpretation of the scriptural witness. In all its aspects, the interpretation of Scripture involves criticism. We ask critical questions of Scripture, e.g.: Does God's liberating word really come to expression in this text? We also find ourselves placed under its criticism, e.g.: Are we really open to the liberating word?

We must interpret Scripture historically, and that necessarily means in terms of the modern critical understanding of history. But is that understanding absolute? Is history more open to the new than our closed schemas of cause and effect allow? Does not the reality of an event also include its future, that toward which it tends?

We must interpret Scripture theocentrically, and that will always mean at first going to Scripture with our inherited or preconceived notions of God. But is this pre-understanding beyond criticism? Are we open to hear the story of a strange God, a God who turns upside down all our prior understandings of divine power and freedom?

We must interpret Scripture contextually, and that will always no doubt begin from the actual personal and social context in which we find ourselves. But is that context one of complacency or one of yearning for freedom? Is it one of isolation and apathy or one of solidarity with the oppressed? If we are to be in a position to hear Scripture as a liberating word of God, must we not expect that our own way of life and our social awareness will have to be reformed and transformed as we recognize our solidarity with a world still groaning to be free?

We have sought to redefine and relocate the authority of Scripture rather than to undercut it. The authority of Scripture is not absolute but instrumental, not intrinsic but functional. Jesus Christ is Lord. He is Lord also of Scripture, and his lordship brings freedom. "Where the Spirit of the Lord is, there is freedom" (II Cor. 3:17).

Because the authority of Scripture is finally the liberating power of its message which centers in Jesus Christ, our rethinking of basic Christian doctrines moves in the next chapter from an interpretation of Scripture as liberating word to an understanding of Jesus as the different liberator.

Chapter 2

Jesus the
Different Liberator

In the preceding chapter we noted some of the ways the witness of Scripture has been taken captive. We discovered that Scripture itself must be liberated from captivity if it is to function as liberating word. If the doctrine of Scripture must be freed from misinterpretations, so also must the doctrine of the person and work of Jesus Christ. The purpose of the present chapter is to interpret Christ as liberator and to understand liberation in the light of Christ.

The liberating word of Scripture converges on the history of a particular human being, Jesus of Nazareth. This person —not a set of religious ideas, ethical norms, or sociopolitical programs—is the foundation of Christian faith. In the words of Hans Küng: What makes Christianity special is that it considers the history of Jesus to be "ultimately decisive, definitive, archetypal" for our relationship with God, with other persons, and with society.[20]

Yet as Küng goes on to say, the unavoidable question is: Which Jesus is decisive for Christian faith and life? Is it the Jesus of piety who offers comfort to the troubled soul? Is it the incarnate Son of God of classical dogma who unites in one person both divine and human natures? Is it the Jesus of Western liberalism who represents the highest ideal of human personality? Is it the Jesus of the radical left and the revolutionaries who ignites movements of liberation from social and political oppression?

Of these possibilities, the description of Jesus as liberator is certainly the most suspect for many people in the church. To some it sounds merely faddish; to others, almost blasphemous. Nevertheless, "Liberator" has become the christological title par excellence in recent liberation theology, especially in black theology and in Latin-American liberation theology.[21]

At least three things can be said in defense of the title Liberator. First, the understandings of Jesus and salvation in the New Testament itself are far from uniform. There is a history of christological titles already in the New Testament, and a rich variety of metaphors is employed by the early church to express the meaning of the saving work of Christ. Jesus is called the Christ, the Son of God, the Son of Man, Lord, and Savior, to mention only the more prominent titles. And his work of salvation is described as a payment of a ransom (Mark 10:45), a victory over the powers of this world (Col. 2:15), a sacrifice (Heb. 10:12), an act of justification (Rom. 5:9), an event of reconciliation (II Cor. 5:18), a liberation from the bondage of the law and of sin (Gal. 5:1; Rom. 6:7). This christological and soteriological pluralism in the New Testament itself points to the possibility and necessity of new understandings of Christ and salvation in different social and cultural situations.

Second, in the New Testament we find the beginnings of a description of Jesus as liberator. This view is implicit in the Synoptic Gospels and becomes explicit in the theology of Paul. For Paul, Jesus has brought freedom from sin, the law, and the powers of this world. Paul is able to summarize the meaning of Christ in the language of freedom: "For freedom Christ has set us free" (Gal. 5:1). Thus the New Testament itself takes the first steps toward interpreting Jesus and his work as an event of liberation.

Third, the title Liberator brings the christological confession of the church into dialogue with the struggles for liberation in the world today. It creates a point of contact between the proclamation of the church and the aspirations and struggles of millions of people caught in various kinds of bondage and oppression. The ecumenical church owes a great debt to black theologians and to Latin-American theologians who have spoken out of concrete situations of oppression and exploitation, and who have challenged Christians everywhere to grapple with the question of the relationship between salvation in Christ and the history of human liberation.

While the understanding of Jesus as liberator is both creative and prophetically powerful, the new christological title can also be misused. Every christological name is potentially both an aid and an obstacle to a right understanding of Jesus and salvation. This point is made in the story of Peter's confession of Jesus as the Christ (Mark 8:27ff.). Jesus rebuked Peter when he resisted the idea that it was necessary for the Christ to suffer and to die. The christological titles of the early Christian community identify Jesus, but in turn and in a more decisive manner, the concrete history of Jesus redefines the titles.[22] If this is true of the title Christ, it is also true of the title Liberator. In the final analysis, it is not our prior understandings of liberation that identify Jesus; rather, it is Jesus who incarnates and clarifies true liberation. Jesus is liberator, but he is the different liberator.

I

The new understanding of Jesus as liberator must be seen against the background of traditional theories of the saving work of Christ. The two most influential of these theories are salvation through incarnation and salvation through satisfaction. Broadly speaking, these have been the dominant understandings of the saving work of Christ in the Eastern and Western churches respectively.[23]

According to incarnational soteriology, salvation is achieved by the union of divine and human natures in the person, Jesus Christ. Classical christology received definitive expression in the formula of Chalcedon, A.D. 451. In this creed the church declared that Jesus Christ is truly divine and truly human, two natures united in one person, without mingling, without change, without division, without separation. This classical doctrine of the person of Christ includes an understanding of what salvation is and how it is achieved. God is infinite and immortal; humanity is finite and mortal. God is beyond change and free from the ravages of sin and evil; humanity in its fallen state is not only subject to change but enslaved to the powers of sin and death. Salvation occurs when God and human life are united in Christ. This union is "hypostatic," which means it happens by the person-constituting grace of God. In the event of incarnation God takes the initiative and assumes our human condition. Estrangement is overcome, and the two worlds of divinity and humanity are reunited.

The most serious weakness of this model of salvation is that the concrete historical life of Jesus plays at best a secondary role. Salvation is achieved at the ontological level rather than being genuinely historical; the content of salvation is not determined by the actual history of Jesus. Since the union of divinity and humanity is achieved in principle with the birth of Christ, the gospel narrative is read as a series of epiphanies of the incarnation. The point of this criticism is not to dismiss the concept of incarnation altogether. Rather it is to say that what we mean by incarnation must be determined by the concrete history of Jesus, by his life, death, and resurrection. The events between the birth and resurrection of Jesus are not ancillary nor merely illustrative; they are constitutive of the identity of Jesus and of the salvation he brings.

In distinction from the emphasis of the Eastern church, Western soteriology has focused on the cross of Christ. It is his death which is salvific. This emphasis finds its classic expression in the thought of Anselm. According to Anselm's doctrine, God and human beings are related like a feudal lord and his serfs. God requires obedience. Sin is an act of disobedience that violates the order of creation and dishonors

God. Since an offense against God is an infinite offense, a human being is not capable of offering the necessary satisfaction. Yet since humanity is the offender, a human being must offer satisfaction. Hence God has become a human being who renders perfect obedience to God. By Jesus' obedience even unto death, the justice of God is satisfied and the honor of God restored. The passion and crucifixion thus become the basic purpose of the incarnation.

Here again there is a constriction of the gospel narrative. The only really essential act of Jesus Christ is his suffering and dying. Anselm states this point bluntly: The Son of God freely decided to become human in order to die.[24] The preaching and healing of Jesus, his compassion for the poor, his clash with the religious and political authorities of his time are passed over as though of minor importance. Kierkegaard spoke as a representative of this Western concentration on the cross of Christ in the often quoted remark: "If the contemporary generation had left behind them nothing but the words, 'We have believed that in such and such a year God appeared among us in the humble figure of a servant, that he lived and taught in our community, and finally died,' it would be more than enough."[25] We may surely wonder, however, whether Kierkegaard's severely reduced christological confession is "more than enough" when measured by the New Testament picture of Jesus who proclaimed release to the captives, befriended the sick, the poor, the outcast, was seen by his enemies as a blasphemer and a political troublemaker, and was finally crucified.

Thus neither the soteriology of incarnation nor that of satisfaction does justice to the concrete history of Jesus as recounted by the Gospels. Admittedly, these models of the salvation wrought by God in Christ contain elements of truth that must not be neglected. As the doctrine of the incarnation rightly insists, salvation is by the grace of God, who is uniquely present in the history of the man Jesus. And as the doctrine of atonement through the death of Jesus emphasizes, the death of Jesus is of decisive significance for our understanding of God, sin, and salvation. Nevertheless, the new understanding of Jesus as liberator brings to light aspects of salvation missing from the previously dominant theological models. The church today must allow itself to be instructed by this new understanding if it is to be faithful to the concrete history of Jesus and sensitive to the struggles of people for liberation from oppression.

II

The Gospels are not objective, scientific biographies. They are narratives of the ministry and passion of Jesus as seen by the earliest believers in the light of his resurrection from the dead. Nevertheless, the humanity of Jesus is not suppressed by the Easter faith of the early church. While New Testament scholars today reject a "quest of the historical Jesus" in the nineteenth-century fashion, there is general agreement that unmistakable characteristics of the person and ministry of Jesus are mediated by the gospel accounts.[26]

Foremost among these characteristics is Jesus' singular freedom for God; in the closest connection with this is his remarkable freedom for others. The word "freedom" occurs only a few times in the Gospels. But this is not a decisive factor in determining the appropriateness of speaking of the unique freedom of Jesus. The proclamation and activity of Jesus portrayed in the Gospels brings to light a new and radical human freedom: Jesus the free man communicates the free grace of God to those in bondage.

1. Jesus was the man free for God and the coming kingdom of God. According to the gospel tradition, the kingdom of God was at the center of the preaching of Jesus. "The time is fulfilled, and the kingdom of God is at hand; repent, and believe in the gospel" (Mark 1:15). The message and ministry of Jesus were motivated by an unconditional commitment to the honor and glory of God, a boundless passion for the coming of God's kingdom of righteousness, joy, and peace.

The complete openness of Jesus to the cause of God in the world was reflected in the petitions of the prayer he taught his disciples: "Our Father who art in heaven, hallowed be thy name. Thy kingdom come. Thy will be done, on earth as it is in heaven" (Matt. 6:9f.). The priority of the reign of God over everything else was evident in all of Jesus' teaching. "Seek first his kingdom and his righteousness, and all these things shall be yours as well" (Matt. 6:33). In his parables, Jesus described the kingdom as the "hidden treasure," the "pearl of great value," for which one gladly gives up everything (Matt. 13:44–46).

The root of Jesus' freedom for God was his childlike trust in the strong and free graciousness of God. He was certain of the beneficence of God who makes the rain to fall on both good and bad (Matt. 5:45), whose love is like that of a father who readily forgives a wayward son and rejoices greatly in his return home (Luke 15:11–32), whose generosity far exceeds the petty and self-centered calculations of how much more one deserves than others (Matt. 20:1ff.). Jesus' use of the intimate word *abba* (translated "father" or even "papa") when speaking of God clearly expressed his confidence that the majestic and transcendent God is gracious and accessible. God is not distant and unapproachable but near and compassionate. While free, sovereign, and holy, God reigns by love. God's sovereignty and freedom are not autocratic and terrifying but merciful and other-affirming.

In his preaching and healing Jesus saw the beginnings of the new era long awaited by the people of Israel. Thus it was a joyous time. God's new age was arriving, as the signs of Jesus' ministry showed. "The blind receive their sight and the lame walk, lepers are cleansed and the deaf hear, and the dead are raised up, and the poor have good news preached to them" (Matt. 11:5). Jesus acted in the power of the Spirit of God which was the Spirit of the new age. His unique freedom was the freedom of God's own Spirit. He was anointed by the Spirit to preach good news to the poor (Luke 4:18), and by the Spirit he cast out demons (Matt. 12:28).

2. Jesus' freedom for God and the coming kingdom was concretely embodied in his freedom for others, especially for the despised, the poor, and the weak. Because Jesus was so completely "the man for God," he was unreservedly "the man for others." "In Jesus Christ," writes Walter Kasper, "we are faced with a new possibility and an actual example of being human, that of living a human life for God and for others."[27] His baptism was an act of solidarity with sinners. He freely associated with people considered by the prevailing religious criteria to be godless and unclean. He proclaimed good news to the poor, calling them blessed because the kingdom of God was coming to them (Luke 6:20). He had table fellowship with tax collectors and sinners (Luke 5:30). Those who slandered him as "a glutton and a drunkard" (Matt. 11:19) were unable to see that his eating and drinking with sinners was a sign of God's liberating grace.

The new freedom of Jesus brought him into conflict with the custodians of the religious law. He challenged every interpretation of the law of God that made it an instrument of human bondage. Thus he healed on the sabbath (Mark 3:1–6) and declared that love of God and love of one's neighbor, rather than legalistic systems, were the essence of the will of God (Mark 12:28–34). In contradiction to the legalistic spirit and its endemic self-righteousness and callousness, Jesus drew the excluded people of society into the sphere of God's grace: the sick, the demon-possessed, women, and foreigners. Although pious Jews refused to have any dealings with Samaritans, Jesus told the story of a Samaritan whose action exemplified the meaning of love for a needy neighbor (Luke 10:29–37). At a time when women were not considered worthy to sit at the feet of a rabbi, Jesus commended Mary, who wished to learn, rather than Martha, who busied herself entirely with household chores (Luke 10:38–42).

Jesus had deep compassion for the misery of the masses and for the individuals who sought his help (Mark 1:41; 6:34; Luke 7:13, etc.). He proclaimed God's forgiveness and thus freed persons from the destructive forces of guilt, self-hatred, and despair. Even the characteristic form of Jesus' teaching, the parable, encouraged the hearer's freedom and imagination. The parables are a noncoercive form of address. What is involved in hearing the parables is not learning an esoteric doctrine but breaking free from bondage to oneself, which denies the grace of God and ignores the needs of others.[28]

Jesus' mission of liberation cannot be compartmentalized as merely spiritual. He forgave sins and he healed. He called his hearers to repentance and he summoned them to a new form of life. He freed people not only from spiritual death but from the fear of death itself. There were political as well as religious implications in his radical freedom for God and for others. His life and death exposed the idolatry of power and wealth and showed the inescapable opposition between true freedom based on the grace of God and the oppressive rule of the powers of this world.

Jesus' solidarity with the poor and the oppressed did not harden into an ideological exclusiveness. He sought to release the wealthy and the self-satisfied from the bondage of their wealth and religious arrogance (Luke 18:9–14; 19:1–10). While Jesus placed himself on the side of the scapegoats of society, he did not create a new category of scapegoat. His partisanship for the poor and the oppressed was free from the spirit of bitterness and revenge. Here, too, the strangeness of the freedom of Jesus is evident.

3. Jesus' call to freedom for God and for others involved risk and great sacrifice. The coming kingdom of God demanded one's unconditional allegiance (Luke 14:26). It cost one's life (Matt. 10:39). The new freedom of Jesus brought him into conflict with the authorities. His claim to have the authority to forgive sin (Mark 2:5; John 8:1–11), his healing of the sick on the sabbath in violation of the sabbath law (Mark 3:1–6), his challenge of the dominant interpretation of the law of God which failed to grasp the essence of the law as love, and more precisely, as love of one's enemy (Matt. 5:43ff.) were threatening and unacceptable. His proclamation of God's grace and nearness turned legalistic understandings

of God upside down. Moreover, while the political charges
against him were false, at a deeper level his liberating activity
did challenge oppression in every form including the political
form that Jews knew so well. The freedom of Jesus for others,
based on God's free grace, aroused the hostility and suspicion
that resulted in his trial and crucifixion as a blasphemer and
an enemy of imperial rule.

III

According to the gospel narratives, the description of the
freedom of Jesus for God and for others is not exhausted by
what he does. His freedom is perfected in what he suffers; he
is tried, tortured, and finally subjected to crucifixion (the
form of execution reserved for slaves and political criminals).
If the liberating ministry of Jesus clarifies the meaning of his
passion and resurrection, his passion and resurrection illumine and consummate his ministry of liberation.

In the history of Christian theology there has been a tendency to obscure the wholeness of the gospel by concentrating
exclusively on one of its elements. As we have already noted,
the most influential theories of the saving work of Christ tend
to sever the incarnation and especially the death of Jesus
from his concrete historical life. Did it make any real difference to the patristic theory of Jesus' victory over the demonic
powers of sin and death, or to Anselm's theory of the satisfaction of divine justice, or to the moral influence theory of
bourgeois liberalism, that Jesus entered into the utmost solidarity with sinners, the outcast, and the poor, and that he had
table fellowship with them? Did it make any real difference
that he blessed the poor and proclaimed liberty to captives,
that he mediated the liberating power of God's forgiveness to
those trapped or excluded by the law, or that the charges
which brought him to trial and execution were blasphemy
and sedition? Speaking of the abstract and speculative treatment of the death of Jesus which has characterized tradi-

tional theories of atonement, George Hendry rightly asks: "Is it not, indeed, almost self-evident that if we are seeking to know how Jesus died for [others] we should begin by looking at how he lived for them? How can we hope to understand the death of Jesus except in the light of the life that it consummated?"[29]

However, the converse is also true. We cannot separate the life of Jesus from its strange double conclusion in the crucifixion and resurrection. If his life interprets his death, it is also true that his death and resurrection are the key to his life. We cannot understand the distinctiveness of his liberating activity except in the light of his liberating passion. The understanding of Jesus as liberator is ruined if it bypasses or minimizes his suffering and death as the signature of his distinctive freedom. But what sense does it make to speak of the passion and death of Jesus as liberating? Three things must be said in answer to this question.

1. Jesus was put to death. He was executed because by his proclamation and enactment of the free grace of God to the poor and powerless he clashed with the defenders of the religious law on the one hand and with the representatives of imperial Roman rule on the other. The spirit of self-righteousness and the spirit of rule by might were both threatened by his message and ministry. Thus they conspired to destroy him as a blasphemer and a rebel. The powers of religion and the state arranged his political-religious murder.

From this perspective the death of Jesus appears as the completely unforeseen and undesired conclusion of his life. It was something tragic which befell him, a catastrophe in view of his audacious claim to forgive sin and to proclaim good news to the poor in anticipation of the advent of the kingdom of God. Seen in this light, his crucifixion appears simply as another instance of the triumph of the powers of this world which hold human beings in bondage. Jesus was a champion of freedom who came to a heroic but tragic end.

2. The gospel narrative, however, does not present the crucifixion as mere historical fate. Jesus' passion and death

were not something that merely happened to him. However questionable historically Jesus' predictions of his passion and death may be in their present form, the conviction that Jesus knew and accepted the danger of his ministry and had intimations of its bitter conclusion is deeply embedded in the gospel tradition. Jesus set his face toward Jerusalem (Luke 9:51). He made himself vulnerable for the sake of God's kingdom. He did not seek to die. He was not in love with death. But he did not avoid the risk of his proclamation and enactment of the new freedom of God's kingdom.

On the other hand, Jesus explicitly refused to adopt a policy of violence to hasten God's kingdom. He thus differed fundamentally with the Zealots on the nature of the kingdom and the power by which it comes. Jesus chose the power of God's weakness over against the ultimate weakness of coercive human power. He chose sacrificial love over revolutionary violence not because he was antirevolutionary but because the revolution of God, which he represented, was radical and total.

Thus the Gospels present the passion and death of Jesus as his free act, as the perfection of his freedom for God and for others. His solidarity with sinners and his comradeship with the poor, the powerless, and all who experience the hell of godforsakenness, was consummated in his death on the cross. Paul describes this final identification of Jesus with the lost as his being made a curse for us (Gal. 3:13), his being made sin for our sake (II Cor. 5:21). The Gospels of Mark and Matthew make a similar affirmation by recounting the cry of dereliction from the cross: "My God, my God, why hast thou forsaken me?" (Mark 15:34). This terrible cry expressed the utmost depth of Jesus' solidarity with a godless world. He became the representative of all who cry from the depths of suffering and despair for the coming of God's kingdom of justice and freedom. The long history of the suffering of Israel, of the weeping of Rachel, Jeremiah, and Job, is included in Jesus' cry from the cross. This cry is not resignation to the inevitable. It is a passionate expostulation with

God, an anguished protest to God, a prayer from the depths of despair, and the experience of the absence of God.

3. According to the gospel narrative, the deepest mystery of the passion and death of Jesus is that in this consummation of his freedom for God and the coming kingdom, God's own love and freedom are decisively present and revealed. Jesus willingly surrendered himself in love to the will of God whom he trusted, in the darkness of death, to be ultimately gracious. Jesus radically entrusted himself, his life, his liberating ministry, to the one he called Father. Easter faith proclaims that God vindicated Jesus by raising him from the dead, thus declaring him to be the personal expression of God's own life and kingdom. The meaning of the resurrection of the crucified Jesus for our understanding of God is this: God was not a distant spectator but was decisively present, speaking, acting, and suffering in all that Jesus did and in all that happened to him. In Jesus' acts of solidarity with the poor and lowly, God acts. In the suffering of Jesus, God suffers. The full force of human alienation, hostility, and injustice are experienced by God in the passion and death of Jesus.

James Cone emphasizes the importance of the presence of God in the cross and resurrection of Jesus: "The theological significance of the cross and resurrection is what makes the life of Jesus more than just the life of a good man who happened to like the poor. *The finality of Jesus lies in the totality of his existence in complete freedom as the Oppressed One, who reveals through his death and resurrection that God himself is present in all dimensions of human liberation.* His death is the revelation of the freedom of God, taking upon himself the totality of human oppression; his resurrection is the disclosure that God is not defeated by oppression but transforms it into the possibility of freedom."[30]

The risen Lord is identical with the crucified Jesus. That means he is the same as the one who befriended sinners and proclaimed liberty to captives and good news to the poor. When the identity of the risen Lord with the crucified Jesus is obscured, the resurrection is readily interpreted in privatis-

tic and spiritualistic ways. This has often happened in the
church's theology and preaching of the resurrection. When
we confess that Jesus is risen, however, we are affirming that
the future of the world belongs to the crucified Lord. We are
declaring that only Jesus the friend of the poor has the right
to rule over the world, that he alone defines the future for
which we hope, that the history of the struggle for freedom,
justice, and peace throughout God's creation has its goal and
criterion in him. In the crucified and risen Jesus "all the
promises of God find their Yes" (II Cor. 1:20).

The rule of this Lord means the radical transformation of
all social and political relationships and the conception of
power they embody. Jesus rules in a way that inverts our
ideas of lordship. He rules as a servant rather than by lording
it over others (Mark 10:42–45). The lordship of Jesus is not
coercive, domineering almightiness but love and friendship
that make others free. Jesus calls himself a friend who gives
his life for others (John 15:13–14). He draws his disciples into
a new world of open friendship with those who are despised
(Luke 7:34). The spirit of friendship opens us to people who
are very different from us. As Jürgen Moltmann put it: "The
friendship of Jesus cannot be lived and its friendliness cannot
be disseminated when friendship is limited to people who are
like ourselves and when it is narrowed down to private life.
. . . Open friendship prepares the ground for a friendly
world."[31] Jesus is the different liberator because he frees us
for this friendship with God and thus for friendship and
solidarity with the poor and the despised of the earth.

IV

When Christians confess that Jesus is liberator, they are
bearing witness that they have found in him the concrete
focus and goal of the liberation movement of God in the
world. To receive by faith the Spirit of the risen Jesus is to
begin to live in the power of the radical freedom for God and

for others that Jesus supremely actualized. Jesus liberates us for friendship and solidarity with others, especially with the despised and the oppressed. This confession is more than a memory and more than a present experience. It is a world-encompassing hope.

The first Christians were oriented to the future. They did not look primarily backward but forward. They lived in anticipation of the fulfillment of the era of freedom and friendship begun in Jesus and actively at work in their lives by the power of his Spirit. When they confessed that God had raised Jesus from the dead, they understood that event as the beginning of the time of liberation for the entire creation. Faith in the resurrection was not the assurance of eternal life for the solitary self. The resurrection of Jesus by God was the "first fruits" of the general resurrection of the dead (I Cor. 15:20). It was the start of the consummation of God's universal kingdom. Similarly, the Spirit of Christ was experienced by the early Christians as the power of God's future, the "first fruits" of God's kingdom (Rom. 8:23), the "guarantee" of the coming fulfillment (II Cor. 1:22).

What would be the features of a community today that lived in the power of this Spirit of freedom and within the horizon of this hope?

1. A Spirit-filled community would be an inclusive community. The liberating Spirit of Jesus creates a truly "catholic" community in which barriers that separate persons from each other are torn down. Such inclusiveness was not achieved definitively in early Christianity so that all we would need to do would be to copy the social life and organization of the early church. Paul did not challenge oppressive social structures of his time such as slavery, Roman tyranny, and the subordination of women in society. No doubt expectation of the imminent end of history discouraged him from extending the implications of freedom in Christ to all social institutions and practices of his time. In one arena, however, Paul understood the liberation of God in Jesus Christ to involve revolutionary social consequences. The hostility and

division between Jew and Gentile had been overcome in Christ. The new friendship of Jews and Gentiles in Christ was a foretaste of God's inclusive kingdom.

The tendency and direction of the new freedom and new friendship in Christ are unmistakable in Paul's declaration: "There is neither Jew nor Greek, there is neither slave nor free, there is neither male nor female; for you are all one in Christ Jesus" (Gal. 3:28). If this is the direction of God's liberating activity in the world, then the church today must see its mission accordingly. Liberated by the one who was friend of the despised and who himself became poor and accursed for our sake, Christians in economically advanced societies will ask what friendship with the poor requires in the present. A church living in the power of the Spirit of Jesus will not only oppose all oppression of people because of sex or race; it will be itself a living experiment in new brotherhood and new sisterhood.

2. A Spirit-filled community would be a community that does not try to evade experiences of suffering and negation. Paul the apostle of Christian freedom preached Christ crucified (I Cor. 1:23) and spoke of sharing the sufferings of Christ (Phil. 3:10).

The relationship between suffering and liberation is not easily understood in the churches of North America. Our church life has been deeply influenced by the ideals of industrial and technological society: the control and exploitation of material and human resources, mastery over nature and history, progress toward a golden age. If our society is "officially optimistic," our churches are often merely the religious wing of this optimistic faith in our powers to make human life secure and happy through improved technique. Not only advanced technological society but the Christian churches in this society are inept in dealing with the experience of radical suffering and negativity.[32]

In calling for a new solidarity with the poor of the earth, what is at stake is not only the humanity of the poor but our own humanity. The gap between the wealthy nations of the

Northern Hemisphere and the poor nations of the Southern Hemisphere continues to widen. Rich Christians need to learn the significance of limits of economic growth and consumption for human life on a finite planet. Learning to curb the desire for more and more is one way in which Christians in affluent societies would respond to the call of Jesus to bear their cross. Authentic liberation and the experience of suffering cannot be separated. The liberation movement of God includes crucifixion as well as resurrection, exile as well as exodus.

3. A Spirit-filled community would be a community that celebrates the liberating grace of God here and now. As Paul instructed, it would rejoice greatly because the Lord is at hand (Phil. 4:4–5).

The liberating Spirit of the crucified Christ is not the spirit of resignation and melancholy. God's new world has established a beachhead in this world. The Spirit of freedom is working in the Christian community and in the world, if often secretly and in the most surprising ways. There are signs of new life, new beginnings both in personal and in communal histories. The Christian community celebrates what God has done and is doing to liberate persons; even now we taste the aperitif of the new age of freedom. Christians are called to experiment in the formation of new patterns of life, to shape institutions and relationships so that they more adequately reflect the kingdom of freedom and justice for which we pray and work.

In the worship of the community there is both rejoicing in the presence of the Spirit of new life and grieving in solidarity with an expectant but still afflicted creation; there is both gratitude for the suffering love of God manifest in Jesus and anguish over the continuing brutalization of human beings and the destruction of nature. Nevertheless, Christian worship "has an unmistakable trend and a clear direction towards the victory of life and the consummation of freedom in God's coming."[33]

V

We have attempted to sketch the distinctive features of the liberating life, death, and resurrection of Jesus. In his history Christian faith sees the decisive embodiment of the liberation movement of God in the world. Jesus frees us for faith in the gracious God, releases us for friendship and solidarity with the poor and the oppressed of the earth, and opens us to creative hope even in the abyss of the experience of suffering and death. This liberating activity of God is for Christians the light in which all other liberation movements have to be seen. Confession of Jesus as liberator establishes both the right of Christians to participate in the liberation movements of our time and the responsibility to do so critically. Critical Christian participation would manifest itself in several ways.

First, in the light of Jesus the liberator, the cause of human liberation must be seen holistically rather than partially. There is a tendency among all liberation movements to claim ultimacy and exclusivity as the vanguard of the future. The question whether sexism or racism is the root cause of human alienation is pointless, for human beings need to be liberated from both. The debate whether exploitative capitalism or totalitarian socialism is the lesser of evils makes little sense, for both political rights and economic justice are essential to the development of free human life in a peaceful society. Liberation movements have a tendency to perpetuate the special-interest and group-bound consciousness that characterizes the old world of oppression. Jesus did not set people free by creating a kind of negative identity. To be sure, there is a partisanship in the ministry and proclamation of Jesus, a partisanship for the poor and the exploited, the sick and the dying, the sinners and the accursed. But this partisanship has the goal of new community. Jesus frees and reconciles. Christians will be characterized by their partisanship for the oppressed, but they will not identify the kingdom of God with the goals of a particular liberation movement. Their partisanship will be critical. "A critical partisanship," writes Peter Hodgson, "is one that is iconoclastic; it challenges and seeks to break the idolatry, ideology, alienation and propaganda that accompany most political movements, whether to the left or the right."[34]

Second, in the light of Jesus the liberator, true liberation means not the exchange of the power over others from one set of masters to another but the transformation of the meaning of power. The passion and death of Jesus at the hands of the established religious and political authorities creates a dangerous memory that stands opposed to all political idolatries, civil religion, nationalism, and militarism. To be crucified with Christ is to be freed from the bondage of these gods. The cross of Christ is the sign of God's identification with the victims of oppression in history. But it is also the expression of God's love which is greater than and different from the power possessed by masters and desired by slaves. Just as Jesus rejected the way of the Zealots, so Christians will resist the temptation to make revolutionary violence a *policy* by which the violence of the oppressors will be overcome. Violence is not always avoidable in the struggle for liberation. But as Paul Lehmann argues, Christians in the midst of revolution will resist the temptation to convert the risk of violence as a last resort into the policy of violence.[35] The spirit of vengeance and indiscriminate violence is totally opposed to the transvaluation of power revealed in the cross of Jesus the liberator. Violence cannot finally be overcome by violence. A more just world cannot be established by the strategies of an unjust world. Thus the process of liberation becomes radical only when it includes the freedom of all people from their own ideologies of power and self-righteousness as well as from their masters and exploiters. "The gospel of liberation is for *all* people. Christ died for 'the many,' and that includes all classes and groups in society."[36]

Third, in the light of Jesus the liberator, the human liberation we seek is acknowledged as a gift as well as a task. We are set free by the grace of God and called to the freedom of service. Freedom begins in joyful receptiveness of God's acceptance and affirmation of us. That is the basis of our call to solidarity with others. Openness to the grace of God is the foundation of active engagement in liberation struggles. Without the joy of the provisional gift of freedom in the Spirit of Christ, the call to promote freedom in the world becomes burdensome and legalistic. This has been the experience of many young people in recent years. If human liberation, including our own, is only a task and not also a gift, then discouragement, resignation, and cynicism eventually triumph. Faith in the lordship of Jesus the liberator is the basis of the joy and confidence of the Christian community. In the power of the Spirit of the crucified and risen Lord, perseverance in the service of God's justice, freedom, and peace is possible.

Our reflections in this chapter on the otherness of the freedom of Jesus remain incomplete until we take a further step in the rethinking of Christian doctrine. If Jesus is not simply another freedom fighter but the concrete expression in a human life of God's way of being free for others, our understanding of God and his relationship to the cause of human liberation will have to be transformed accordingly. As I shall show in the following chapter, the doctrine of the Trinity articulates this radically different conception of God.

Chapter 3

The Trinity
and Human Liberty

If we call Scripture the Word of God because it is a genuinely liberating word, and if we see the decisive expression of the liberating activity of God in the crucified and risen Jesus, our customary ideas of God will be shaken to the foundations.

The church's experience of such a shaking is formulated in the doctrine of the Trinity. Christians speak of God who is Father, Son, and Holy Spirit. This trinitarian name marks a revolution in our understanding of God. Our task in this chapter is to clarify the relationship between faith in the triune God and the process of liberation.

Stated negatively, the Christian meaning of the word "God" is not identical with whatever happens to be called divine in human experience or in the various spheres of culture. The God of the gospel is not just another name for our highest ideals and values. As long as God remains for us a vague and nameless reality, we define divinity arbitrarily on the basis of our self-images and our social ideologies. There is good reason, therefore, to heed Calvin's warning to contemplate God as Father, Son, and Holy Spirit lest "only the bare and empty name of God flits about in our brains, to the exclusion of the true God."[37]

The early church, the medieval church, the church of the Reformation, all confessed their faith in the triune God. Up to the modern period, the name of Father, Son, and Holy Spirit was held by Christians to be the only name consistent with God's self-identification in the history of the crucified Lord and in the life-transforming presence of the Holy Spirit. Liberal Protestant theology, however, considered the doctrine of the Trinity more or less burdensome and dispensable. Trinitarian theology was dismissed as arbitrary speculation with no essential relationship to the central Christian message.

The eclipse of the doctrine of the Trinity in much of modern theology has been matched by its declining importance in the everyday life of Christian believers. While trinitarian language is still used in worship services, in the administration of baptism, and in some prayers and hymns, for many Christians this language is surrounded by an impenetrable cloud. They look upon trinitarian doctrine as dark and confusing, and in any case of no real significance for Christian faith and practice. The doctrine of the Trinity is widely thought to be a "kind of higher theological mathematics for the initiated."[38] When this attitude prevails, confession of the triune God becomes mere authoritarian belief and mindless repetition. Dietrich Bonhoeffer rightly criticized the church and theology for presenting doctrines like the Trinity to people and saying in effect, "like it or lump it."[39]

We need to take a fresh look at the doctrine of the Trinity. We need to recover its basis in the gospel of the crucified Lord, its centrality for Christian faith and life, and its implications for the social witness of the church. Above all, we need to probe the relationship between faith in the triune God and the human struggle for freedom. As I shall contend, the doctrine of the Trinity points beyond the modern denial of God in the name of human freedom on the one hand and the oppressive, imperialistic understandings of God embedded in much of the theological tradition on the other. The triune God is not the enemy but the foundation of true human freedom.

I

The doctrine of the Trinity cannot be derived from Scripture through proof texts. The scriptural basis of the doctrine is deeper and less obvious than that suggested by a simple collection of texts such as the Great Commission (Matt. 28:19) and the apostolic benediction (II Cor. 13:14). Far from lying on the surface of Scripture, the doctrine of the Trinity is the product of three or four centuries of experience, reflection, and debate in the church. It is a response to the question: How is God to be identified in the light of the history of Jesus Christ and the transforming presence of his Spirit?

The patristic church answered this question by using philosophical categories available at the time. Of course, this creates problems of understanding for us. As an interpretation of Scripture, the doctrine of the Trinity must now itself be interpreted. But it is naive to fault the church for not simply repeating the words of Scripture. Since the controversy about God centered precisely on how Scripture was to be interpreted, it was impossible simply to quote Scripture in a parrotlike fashion. That would have been an evasion of the question.

The classical trinitarian formulas are familiar. In A.D. 325 the Council of Nicaea declared Jesus Christ the Son of God to be of "one substance" *(homoousios)* with God the Father. In A.D. 381 the Council of Constantinople also affirmed the divinity of the Holy Spirit: the Spirit is "Lord," "giver of life," the one "who spoke through the prophets" and who is to be worshiped and glorified together with the Father and the Son. By the early fifth century, through the efforts of Athanasius and the Cappadocian fathers in the East and especially Augustine in the West, trinitarian doctrine was firmly established. According to this doctrine, God is "one substance in three persons." The Father eternally begets the Son, and from the Father and the Son proceeds the Holy

Spirit. The unity of the three was emphasized by the doctrine of coinherence *(perichōresis)*. Father, Son, and Spirit are not separate and independent "persons" in the modern sense, but each interpenetrates the others and has a distinctive existence only in relation to the others.

Such language is obviously removed from the apostolic preaching of Christ crucified and risen for our salvation. The point of the doctrine of the Trinity, however, is not simply to repeat the gospel and certainly not to replace it. It is an interpretation of the gospel as it bears on the Christian understanding of God and of the kingdom of God. The doctrine of the Trinity identifies God and the coming kingdom in the light of the history of Jesus Christ and the coming of his liberating, life-giving Spirit. It redefines the power of God and the presence of God. The power of God is defined as the self-imparting love of the crucified Christ and the presence of God is understood as the re-creating, liberating, reconciling Spirit of Christ at work in the world as the "first fruits" (Rom. 8:23) of God's coming kingdom.

As heir of Old Testament faith, the early church understood God to be the Creator who comes to establish righteousness throughout the world. God is not an abstract and lifeless transcendent ideal. God is the one who comes to bring justice, freedom, and peace on earth. According to the New Testament, the coming of God to rule is defined by the history of Jesus Christ and by the presence of his life-transforming Spirit. The primary function of the doctrine of the Trinity is to speak of God not as a lifeless absolute but as a living history which must be narrated.

In Jesus' forgiveness of sinners, in his proclamation of good news to the poor, in his healing of the sick and casting out of demons, in his table fellowship with the despised, the kingdom of God draws near. But for the New Testament community it is the crucifixion which brings Jesus' history of forgiving and self-giving love to completion. The apostle Paul describes the crucifixion both as God's surrendering or giving up of his Son for our sake (Rom. 8:32) and as the Son of

God's surrender of himself in obedient love to the will of the Father (Gal. 1:3–4). Thus in the history of Jesus which comes to its awesome conclusion in his crucifixion, Jesus and his Father both act in self-giving, suffering love for the salvation of the world. In the ministry and passion of Jesus the kingdom of God comes, but in a strange and unexpected form.

According to the New Testament witness, however, the divine history of love does not stop with the crucifixion of Jesus. The love of God is triumphant and radiates into human life. The provisional triumph of God's love is the resurrection of Jesus from the dead. The radiation of this love is the coming of the Spirit who brings new life, new freedom, new hope to those in bondage. The doctrine of the Trinity defines God as "the radiating event of love."[40] If according to the history of Jesus the coming God is the crucified God, then according to the activity of his Spirit the coming God is the life-giving, liberating God. God is the one "who raised Christ Jesus from the dead" (Rom. 8:11; Gal. 1:1) and who has sent the Spirit of love and freedom into our hearts (Rom. 5:5; II Cor. 3:17). God is present now as the Spirit of resurrection, the Spirit who brings life (Rom. 8:11), the Spirit who liberates human beings from bondage to the law, sin, and death. The Spirit of God is none other than the Spirit of the crucified and risen Lord. Life in the Spirit is the commencement of the universal triumph of God's kingdom.

Thus as an interpretation of the biblical witness to the identity of God and the kingdom, the doctrine of the Trinity is far from an exercise in speculative curiosity. It is, if anything, antispeculative in intent. It wants to describe God not in terms of metaphysical abstractions but in terms of a history, the history of the mutual self-giving love of Father and Son, and of the coming of the life-giving Spirit of their love. God's being is not static but dynamic and processive. The reality of God is a living movement of self-giving love that liberates human life and creates new community. God is the "event of suffering, liberating love."[41] This is the identity of

God which the classical doctrine of the Trinity, for all its historically conditioned conceptuality, safeguards against oppressive, sub-Christian conceptions of God.

II

The doctrine of the Trinity constitutes a revolution in our understanding of God. Insofar as it intends to be an interpretation of the New Testament message, it affirms that God is majestic self-giving love that liberates.

Ordinarily we think of God or the gods in terms of superior power. The power we ascribe to God is controlling, dominating power. God is whatever power we think can destroy us or make us powerful. Many things can function in our life as gods: nation, race, sex, drugs, material wealth. Such realities are just as truly gods for people today, however secular they may imagine themselves to be, as were Zeus and Athena for the ancient Greeks. God's powerfulness, as we ordinarily conceive it, is a reflection of the will-to-power manifest in our lives as individuals and in our social structures. The gods to whom we bow are our egocentric and ethnocentric selves writ cosmically large. As Barth said, we try to speak of God by speaking of ourselves in a loud voice. The result is that we define not God but the demonic.

Modern atheism is a protest against the conception of God as power which enslaves and crushes human life. The Marxist humanist Ernst Bloch sees the God of established Christianity as the reflection of the domination of the poor by the rich, and calls for the "detheocratizing" of the Bible and of the Judeo-Christian tradition. Bloch's criticism of traditional Christian theism is to a large extent justified. The triune God, however, is wholly other than the God rejected by modern atheism.

To speak of God as triune is to redefine the power of God in the most radical way. If God is self-giving love that creates community in freedom, then God is not the will-to-power but the will-to-fellowship. God's being is in self-giving. If God is really present in Jesus, in his weakness, suffering, and death, then as H. Richard Niebuhr writes:

> How strangely we must revise in the light of Jesus Christ all our ideas of what is really strong in this powerful world. The power of God is made manifest in the weakness of Jesus, in the meek and dying life which through death is raised to power. We see the power of God over the strong of earth made evident not in the fact that he slays them, but in his making the spirit of the slain Jesus unconquerable. . . . We cannot come to the end of the road of our rethinking the ideas of power and omnipotence. . . . [God's] power is made perfect in weakness and he exercises sovereignty more through crosses than through thrones.[42]

It is this revolution in our understanding of the power of God, and correspondingly in our understanding of creative human power, which we acknowledge when we confess the triunity of God. The power and glory of the triune God is not self-enhancing power and self-aggrandizing glory but self-giving love and shared glory. This is the power that God exercises in relation to us because it is the very same power that defines God eternally as Father, Son, and Holy Spirit. The doctrine of the Trinity is the consistent development of the declaration of Paul that the power of God is Christ crucified for us (I Cor. 1:23–25) and of the simple but inexhaustibly rich Johannine affirmation: "God is love" (I John 4:8).

Arius, a fourth-century theologian, contested this understanding of the power of God. According to Arius, Christ is only a creature of God, albeit the first and greatest of the creatures. In Christ, God is not personally present. God is subject to no limitations and certainly not to suffering and death. Hence the reality of God is greater than what is expressed in Jesus, even if Jesus does mediate knowledge of God and salvation to us. Clearly, Arius did not wish to demean God. On the contrary, the Arian view of God was the most exalted imaginable. For Arius, God is absolute, utterly transcendent, totally free, completely unconditioned power. Arthur McGill aptly describes this position:

> In all the history of Christianity there has hardly been so sophisticated, so Biblically grounded, so thoroughgoing a theology of God's transcendence as that developed by Arius and his followers. Their whole concern was to honor God by setting him above and in contrast to his creatures. They sought to preserve the glory of God by divesting his reality of all those weaknesses and deficiencies which mark his creatures, and by giving him the most absolute kind of mastery over his creatures.[43]

In short, Arius upheld the "infinite qualitative difference" between God and humanity. His doctrine of God was impressive when measured by ordinary conceptions of power. But what did his teaching really come down to? A declaration that divinity—genuine, full divinity—cannot be shared; that God ceases to be God if limited in any way by another. By definition, the being and power of God cannot be communicated to another. Where absolute power is shared, it is no longer absolute, i.e., divine power. Limitation and vulnerability are signs of weakness and hence cannot be attributed to God. God is invulnerable, wholly self-contained, fully complete apart from any other being. The freedom of the God of Arius is absolute. But the God of Arius cannot love. It is simply inconceivable that this God should be identified by the passion of Christ.

Nicene theology, defended especially by Athanasius, represented a completely different conception of God. The quality that constitutes the divinity of the God of the gospel is not absoluteness, incommunicability or invulnerability. The God of the gospel is defined in the act of self-giving love. What makes God worshipful is not the property of absoluteness but the act of being for others, the freedom to love. The biblical proclamation of God's love for us in Jesus Christ, and decisively in his passion and death, requires us to understand the reality of God as open, vulnerable, self-giving love. This is the basic evangelical motive of the Nicene declaration that Jesus Christ is "one substance" with the Father, that the Father from all eternity "begets" a Son, that the Father does not monopolize divine life but shares it eternally with another.

The Arian conception of God is very much alive. As we noted earlier, Marxist humanists like Ernst Bloch criticize the ideas of God that merely serve to disguise our power-hungry, monopolistic, exploitative social attitudes and structures. This criticism exposes an established Christianity in which, liturgical formulas notwithstanding, Arianism has triumphed. Worship of a God whose freedom and power are arbitrary and unlimited makes us and the societies in which we live inhuman.

Karl Barth, leader of the Confessing Church in Germany in its struggle against Hitler, saw Nazism as a secular expression of the perennial heresy of godalmightiness. Praise of the sheer almightiness of God, of the capricious freedom of God, is only a projection of our own will-to-power. When we understand the power of God as the power of a Byzantine emperor magnified infinitely, we completely distort the biblical message. The power of God is not alien, coercive, inhuman, and destructive. "Perhaps you recall," Barth writes, "how when Hitler used to speak about God, he called Him 'the Almighty.' But it is not 'the Almighty' who is God; we cannot understand from the standpoint of a supreme concept of power, who God is. And the person who calls 'the Almighty' God misses God in the most terrible way."[44]

The doctrine of the Trinity is thus an attack on all conceptions of God as absolute power and absolute freedom. It is an assault on "that Arian feeling of reverence for the absolute which lies in the heart of every [human being]."[45] As Barth's theological and political struggle against the godalmightiness of Hitler makes clear, the revolution in the understanding of God represented by trinitarian faith has profound consequences for our social and political orders as well as for our personal lives. The trinitarian understanding of God opposes every theological legitimation of imperial monarchy and the exercise of absolute power in the political sphere. If God is defined not as absolute power but as self-giving love decisively expressed in the cross of Christ, then trinitarian Christian faith is a rejection of all political absolutism and reign by terror. The doctrine of the Trinity has the potential of playing a liberating role in the political and economic struggles of our time by exposing the idolatry of monarchical power and the control and consumption of the world's resources by a few at the expense of the many. Trinitarian faith in God tends in the direction of political and economic theory and practice based on mutuality, participation, and the distribution of power and wealth.[46]

III

If the New Testament identifies God in terms of the mutual self-giving love of Father and Son that culminates in the death of Jesus on the cross, it also identifies God in terms of the resurrection of Jesus from the dead and the liberating presence of the Spirit of resurrection and new life. According to classical trinitarian doctrine, the Spirit too is divine, proceeding from the Father and the Son. The Spirit of love binds together Father and Son and with them forms a perfect community of love in freedom.

The doctrine of the Spirit is probably subject to more arbitrary interpretations than any other Christian doctrine. The Nicene fathers themselves said relatively little about the identity and work of the Spirit. They affirmed simply that the Spirit was "the Lord," "the life giver," and the one "who spoke through the prophets." In modern Christianity the experience of the Spirit is mostly a private affair. It is associated simply with the individual's own appropriation of the message of forgiveness, the granting of spiritual gifts, and the hope of eternal life. Moreover, the activity of the Spirit is virtually severed from the suffering love of God disclosed in the cross of Christ. The result of this is a sensationalistic theology of the Spirit that concentrates on such phenomena as speaking in tongues.

Paul combated views of the Spirit akin to these in his churches. When possession of such gifts as speaking in tongues became the central interest of the Corinthians, Paul countered with the reminder that the Spirit was the Spirit of the crucified Lord and showed itself in loving concern for others. The Spirit for Paul was no mere influx of vitality and power into human life but was intimately bound to the self-giving love of God in Jesus Christ crucified. Furthermore, with his emphasis on the Spirit as the "first fruits" of salvation and his doctrine of the resurrection of the dead as the final moment in the drama of God's liberation of the entire creation, Paul opposed all individualizing and privatizing of the experience of the Spirit. The Spirit brings not only freedom from the bondage of sin, the law, and death, but freedom for others. To be enlivened by the Spirit is to participate in God's liberation of the entire creation for new life in community.

The social and eschatological dimensions of the doctrine of the Trinity were obscured by the preference for the "psychological analogy" in Western trinitarian theology since Augustine. According to the psychological analogy, the trinitarian constitution of the human psyche—memory, understanding, will—is a reflection in human life of the triunity of God. Augustine's description of such "traces of the Trinity" *(vestigia trinitatis)* in human selfhood no doubt promoted deeper understanding of the complex integrity of the human spirit. At the same time, it cast little light on the theological basis of human sociality.

The "social analogy" of the Trinity is needed to correct and complement the psychological analogy. In distinction from the psychological analogy, which focuses on the dynamic unity of psychic activities, the social analogy looks to the phenomenon of persons in relationship for a clue to the mystery of the divine life.

The isolated ego does not constitute human personhood. As John Macmurray argues: "The personal is constituted by personal relatedness. The unit of the personal is not the 'I' but the 'You and I.' "[47] Thus person and community are correlative terms, even if in common experience they are constantly in tension or even conflict with each other. The doctrine of the Trinity challenges our individualistic conceptions of personhood. It defines the divine life as the mutual love of Father, Son, and Spirit. The triune God is not the basis of the absolute ego but the foundation of personal life in community. The being of God is characterized by the perfect giving and receiving of love.

As the affirmation of the sociality of God, the doctrine of the Trinity points to a new understanding of freedom, divine and human. If person and community are correlative terms, so also are the freedom of the individual and life in community. God is perfect community in freedom. In Barth's words, God is the one who loves in freedom. The Spirit of God is the Spirit of love which liberates. Perfect love allows another to be and rejoices in the particularity of the other. The distinguishing mark of the Spirit of God is the emergence of a community in which love and freedom are conjoined.

The modern atheistic attack on God as the enemy of human freedom is right in relation to every idea of God that divorces divine power from love and freedom. The God of the gospel, however, is not antihuman. The triune God is the divine history of self-giving, liberating love making possible genuine human freedom with and for others. Within the history of this God we are defined as persons in community. True freedom is not absolute autonomy any more than genuine community requires the suppression of individuality and diversity in the name of the state.

It is on the basis of a trinitarian understanding of God that Juan Luis Segundo criticizes the image of God that is reflected in the oppressive social and economic structures of the affluent nations of the world. For Segundo, trinitarian theology speaks of God as a community of love; this idea of God

is liberating because it stands in radical opposition to existing
society. Thus the trinitarian definition of God "is an impetus
to implement new and more humane social initiatives that go
far beyond the existing order." The trinitarian history of God
empowers and guides the effort of the church to fashion a
human society which like the divine society would be "con-
cordant by virtue of community, neither confused nor di-
vided, in such a way that the good of one is the good of all,
because the needs and hopes of one touch upon the needs and
hopes of all."[48]

IV

The doctrine of the Trinity, we have contended, must be
approached not speculatively but evangelically. If we are to
avoid arbitrary speculation, we must inquire first not about
the immanent Trinity or the inner life of God but about the
economic Trinity or God manifested to us in the work of
salvation.

Our starting point must be the witness of the New Testament to the coming of the Lord of the world: in the self-giving
love of Jesus who was crucified, in the resurrection of this
Jesus from the dead, and in the coming of his liberating
Spirit.

The biblical God is a dynamic, living reality. God is a
movement, a history, a procession. As Eberhard Jüngel
writes, God's being is "a becoming peculiar to his own
being."[49] God "becomes" by reaching out to us in self-
expending love that liberates. This historical "becoming" of
God does not contradict but reliably expresses God's eternal
way of being. The economic Trinity is the immanent Trinity.[50]

Therefore, in retrospect we confess that God is a
trinitarian history, a trinitarian becoming not only in relation
to us but also in the inner life of God from all eternity. This
retrospective way of speaking about the triune God has its

theological importance and legitimacy. Eternally and really, not temporarily and only in appearance, God the Father generates the Son, and the mutual love of Father and Son issues in the Spirit of communion in freedom. God does not need to create the world in order to become the one who loves in freedom. God is not dependent on the world in the way that the world is dependent on God. God creates the world out of the fullness of love. Thus, speaking of the Trinity in retrospect has the aim of affirming that God's own inner life is a history of liberating love and hence that God is eternally open to the world. If God is not related to the world by fate, neither is the life of God closed like a circle. From all eternity the triune God is open to a history of suffering, liberating love with the world.

Traditionally, theology has emphasized one-sidedly this retrospective way of thinking about the Trinity. The logic of trinitarian thought has been disproportionately backward in direction. That is, theology has concluded backward from God's dealings with us to the Trinity before creation. As Jürgen Moltmann has argued, however, it is important also to think of the Trinity in prospect. The trinitarian history of God moves forward to a consummation symbolized as the kingdom of God. This consummation is of cosmic dimensions. Paul says that all creation is yearning for the coming of the "glorious liberty of the children of God" (Rom. 8:21).

While the world and its liberation are not necessary *a priori* to the life of God, nevertheless by God's own free decision the history and glory of God have been bound up with the liberation of the world through the Spirit of the crucified Lord. The trinitarian God wills to be glorified only as the creation is set free from all forms of bondage and oppression. The history of God is not complete until the kingdom of community in freedom is fully realized. As Moltmann writes: "God is not perfect if this means that he did not in the craving of his love want his creation to be necessary to his perfection. . . . God comes to his glory in that creation becomes free."[51]

The church is not the realized kingdom of God. The mission of the church is to participate in the trinitarian history of God, to let itself be an agent of the self-giving love of God that sets people free. This is the theological basis of the church's involvement in the liberation of human beings from the many forms of bondage and oppression they experience. The church does not need to make imperialistic and exclusive claims to be the only community by which the cause of human freedom is advanced. To be sure, the church is a distinctive community. In its concern for justice, freedom, and peace, in its solidarity with the poor and the oppressed, the church does not receive its primary motivation from the latest liberation movement. The mission of the church is defined by the trinitarian history of God. Nevertheless, there is no reason for the church to be ungrateful and uncooperative in its relationship with other movements seeking a fuller actualization of human freedom. That the Spirit moves where it will should cause Christians to be grateful and modest rather than petty and arrogant. In its trinitarian faith and way of life, the church bears witness to a power at work in human life and history that makes for community in freedom and that will ultimately prevail over all the forces that degrade and enslave God's creatures.

V

If the Christian understanding of God is essentially trinitarian, Christianity contains within itself an atheistic protest. Christians refuse to think and speak of God as a dominative power that at best expresses love only in the counterfeit form of patronization and "charity." The atheistic protest against a God who is the enemy of human freedom is not only theologically legitimate but necessary. At the same time, Christians reject the religion of atheists whose de facto "God" is either the individual self and its unlimited aggrandizement or the authoritarian state and its goals.

We do not rightly grasp the significance of the development of trinitarian faith and doctrine if we fail to see its continuous, disturbing criticisms of our established notions of God and our established ways of life. Knowledge of God and knowledge of ourselves go hand in hand. Doctrines of God and theories of society influence each other. The result of this correlation may be liberating or it may be oppressive. As Segundo states, "Some sort of degradation of [humanity] lies buried within every deformation in our idea of God."[52] Every view of what it means to be human implies a certain understanding of what is divine, and every understanding of what is divine issues in a particular view of what it means to be human.

The theological task is therefore always twofold. One task is to examine critically our doctrine of God to see if it is genuinely biblical and evangelical, i.e., trinitarian. In the light of the reality of God made known to us in the crucified Jesus and his Spirit of freedom, our understanding of God must be emancipated again and again from distorted images. Metaphysical definitions of God as absolute, solitary, immutable, omnipotent are deeply intertwined with our egocentric ways of life and our oppressive social orders. Such conceptions of God support rather than challenge human bondage and misery. The doctrine of the Trinity is indeed a revolution in our understanding of God, for it speaks of God as a history of suffering, liberating, community-forming love.

The other theological task is to examine critically our human forms of life in the light of the God attested by the gospel and affirmed by the doctrine of the Trinity. As Joseph Bracken has pointed out, when God is understood as essentially social, as a community of self-imparting, liberating love, "then human beings will perhaps recognize more readily that they too have a basically social orientation, that the perfection of their nature lies in interdependence with others for the achievement of common goals, not in some unattainable ideal of independence and self-sufficiency."[53]

Christian life is a participation in the history of the triune

God who is free to love and who freely loves. It is a process of being formed in the likeness of Christ by the power of his Spirit. With this trinitarian understanding of God and of Christian life as a background, we turn in the next chapter to a critique of traditional Christian spirituality and to a reformulation of Christian freedom as freedom for others.

Chapter 4

A Spirituality
of Liberation

Let us briefly review the road we have traveled. In Chapter 1 we began with a restatement of the doctrine of the authority of Scripture. We described Scripture as the decisive witness to God's liberating activity. Several principles of interpretation were proposed to guard the integrity and strangeness of this scriptural witness. In Chapter 2 we turned to the gospel narratives and their portrayal of the astonishing freedom of Jesus for God and for others. We contended that our preconceptions about freedom should not be allowed to define Jesus; rather he defines what it means to be free. Then in Chapter 3 we reexamined the Christian doctrine of God so as to clarify the ultimate foundations of freedom. We interpreted trinitarian doctrine to affirm that the God made known in Jesus Christ through his Spirit is the basis of authentic human freedom in community with others.

The restatements of central Christian doctrines offered in the preceding chapters may intrigue some readers and deeply trouble others. Doesn't all this talk of liberation lead to a politicizing of the gospel? Doesn't liberation theology disregard the intensely personal nature of being a Christian: the experience of God's forgiveness, the personal relationship with Christ, the practice of prayer and the other disciplines of Christian life? Doesn't liberation theology ignore the importance of spirituality?[54]

The assumption behind these questions is that spirituality and liberation represent irreconcilable understandings of what Christianity is all about. Spirituality connotes a regimen of devotional exercises followed with the aim of becoming a more deeply religious individual. According to critics, spiritual persons are so preoccupied with the cultivation of their own religious life that they are indifferent to great issues and conflicts in the social and political realms. Liberation, by contrast, immediately brings to mind social and political struggles. It names the process by which oppressed people begin to question and to combat economic exploitation, racial and sexual discrimination, and the violation of basic human rights. Again according to critics, persons so engaged have little interest in prayer and the Bible. Unfortunately, there is more than a little truth in these stereotypes. This is why for some years many churches have been polarized between the defenders of spirituality and the advocates of liberation as the highest expression of Christian commitment.

Can this dichotomizing of Christian discipleship be overcome? This is one of the questions raised by Gustavo Gutiérrez in his book *A Theology of Liberation*. He writes: "There is great need for a spirituality of liberation."[55] This phrase describes the new experience of Latin-American Christians who have begun to participate actively in the cause of full human liberation in their lands oppressed by poverty and the denial of elementary human rights. Precisely because of their involvement, these Christians find themselves in need not only of new theological understanding but of a new spirituality. While emphasizing that rigorous theological reflection on the struggles for liberation is indispensable, Gutiérrez nevertheless insists that new theological vision and the development of new theological categories are not enough. "We need a vital attitude, all embracing and synthesizing, informing the totality as well as every detail of our lives; we need a 'spirituality.' "[56]

According to Gutiérrez, traditional spirituality is estranged from the struggle against oppression in the world today and too often fosters only "childish attitudes, routine and escapes."[57] The result is that for many Christians in Latin America, "the participation in the process of liberation causes a wearying, anguished, long and unbearable dichotomy between their life of faith and their revolutionary commitment."[58] Gutiérrez contends that this dichotomy is detrimental both to the life of faith and to the cause of liberation. The struggle for the liberation of human life in its political and socioeconomic dimensions and the gift of new life and freedom in Christ are not separate but interpenetrating processes. Their interpenetration requires both that we transcend every reductionism in understanding the liberation process and that we move toward a radically new kind of Christian spirituality.

The importance of Gutiérrez' call to a new spirituality is not limited to the Latin-American situation. The possibility of a spirituality of liberation breaks through the deadening alternatives so familiar in churches everywhere: prayer or politics; transformation of individuals or transformation of social conditions; a personal or a political interpretation of the gospel. The call to a spirituality of liberation challenges Christians in affluent countries to raise very disturbing questions about themselves and their ecclesial way of life. What sort of spirituality dominates the churches in North America? Could a spirituality of liberation ever take root in them? What would be the conditions of the emergence of this new spirituality?

I

An intimation of what the development of a new Christian spirituality might involve within North American experience is found in Mark Twain's *Huckleberry Finn.* If there ever was a person who wanted to be free, it is Huck. He runs away from home and his drunkard father. He flees from the efforts of Widow Douglas and Miss Watson to tame and civilize him. He takes to the river and to life on a raft. Without doubt, the story of Huckleberry Finn is the story of a pilgrim in search of freedom.

On his pilgrim way, Huck meets the runaway slave, old black Jim. Like Huck, Jim wants to be free. Whereas Huck is fleeing from the efforts of the dominant culture to make him conform to its rules and values, Jim is fleeing from his condition as a slave within that same society. The two journey together down the river. Their relationship grows and deepens. Even while he enjoys Jim's companionship, Huck at first plays some mean tricks on him. On one occasion this results in Jim's being severely bitten by a snake. At another point in their journey, the two are separated for a long period of time. Huck, off on one of his adventures, almost completely forgets Jim. But their friendship grows, their lives intertwine, and their separate quests for freedom become quietly and gradually a single quest.

A major crisis develops when Huck has to decide whether to inform Jim's owner where the old slave may be found. Huck's conscience torments him. He tries to pray for help, but the words will not come. He has been thoroughly trained to think that the right thing to do is to tell where Jim is hiding so that he can be returned to his lawful owner. Surely his Sunday school teachers would have insisted that he tell on Jim. Surely God would want Huck to do that, and if he didn't he would most probably go to hell. After all, Jim was a black man, and he was someone's property. No wonder Huck couldn't pray. His obligation was as plain as day. "You can't pray a lie," Huck says.

> So I was full of trouble, full as I could be; and didn't know what to do. At last I had an idea; and I says, I'll go and write the letter—and *then* see if I can pray. Why, it was astonishing, the way I felt as light as a feather right straight off, and my troubles all gone. So I got a piece of paper and a pencil, all glad and excited, and set down and wrote:

Miss Watson, your runaway nigger Jim is down here two mile below Pikesville, and Mr. Phelps has got him and he will give him up for the reward if you send.

Huck Finn

I felt good and all washed clean of sin for the first time I had ever felt so in my life, and I knowed I could pray now. But I didn't do it straight off, but laid the paper down and set there thinking—thinking how good it was all this happened so, and how near I come to being lost and going to hell. And went on thinking. And go to thinking over our trip down the river; and I see Jim before me all the time: in the day and in the nighttime, sometimes moonlight, sometimes storms, and we a-floating along, talking and singing and laughing. But somehow I couldn't seem to strike no places to harden me against him, but only the other kind. I'd see him standing my watch on top of his'n, 'stead of calling me, so I could go on sleeping . . . ; and would always call me honey, and pet me, and do everything he could think of for me, and how good he always was; and at last I struck the time I saved him by telling the men we had smallpox aboard, and he was so grateful, and said I was the best friend old Jim ever had in the world, and the *only* one he's got now; and then I happened to look around and see that paper.

It was a close place. I took it up, and held it in my hand. I was a-trembling, because I'd got to decide, forever, betwixt two things, and I knowed it. I studied a minute, sort of holding my breath, and then says to myself: "All right, then, I'll go to hell" —and tore it up.[59]

This is a remarkable description of the breakdown of an old spirituality and the painful coming to birth of what Gutiérrez calls a new spirituality of liberation. According to the old spirituality, sin would be defined in such prohibitions as: Do not drink, do not smoke, do not tell lies, and most emphatically do not harbor a fugitive slave. Nurtured in this sort of spirituality, Huck necessarily experiences a conflict between the life of prayer and faith in God on the one hand

and his concern for the freedom of another human being on the other hand.

Huck experiences a conversion, but what a conversion it is! He is converted to his neighbor. He comes to see that the freedom he wills for himself he must also will for others. He cannot be free unless Jim is also free. Huck's freedom and Jim's freedom are inseparable. In order to reach this tremendous spiritual insight, Huck has to go against all the morality and religious doctrine he has been taught. He commits himself to helping Jim become free even if it means, in terms of his religious training, having to go to hell.

This episode in the spiritual life of Huckleberry Finn is poignant. Did Huck ever come to a new understanding of prayer? Did he arrive at a new perception of the relationship between faith in God and commitment to the cause of human freedom? We are not told. Mark Twain's concern in this passage is to show the bankruptcy of the spirituality dominant in the churches of his day, and he does this with extraordinary power and eloquence.

II

Mark Twain's description of the collision between conventional North American spirituality and human liberation makes us painfully aware of the continuing crisis of spirituality in our churches. The existing expressions of Christian spirituality among us are largely alienating and almost entirely privatistic. They are narrowly focused on the salvation of the solitary soul rather than on the coming of God's kingdom. They are divorced from the struggles for justice, freedom, and peace in our society and around the world. The self that is the center of these spiritualities is an asocial and an ahistorical middle-class self. There is little awareness of the corporate and relational meanings of salvation, rebirth, and new creation that are present in the biblical witness. To be in Christ is not to be set free to be a self in the privatistic sense; it is to be liberated by the love of God from the power of egocentricity which estranges us from God and from others. Yet many current forms of Christian spirituality seem to cut Christians off from others rather than binding them to ever-widening circles of human need and hope.

A Christian spirituality is a particular way of cultivating full human freedom under the dominion of the Spirit of Christ, a process of growing into mature personhood in Christ (Eph. 4:13). It is a process of entering ever more deeply into a new way of life in relationship with God and in solidarity with others. At the center of Christian spirituality has always been the experience of being forgiven by God, uniting with Christ by faith, maturing into his likeness, participating in his death, and sharing in the power of his resurrection. Christian life is nourished in a community of believers who listen for the Word of God, celebrate the Sacraments, pray for the coming of God's kingdom, and serve others. The spiritual pilgrimage of the Christian is a movement away from the old self-enclosed life toward a new way of life in fellowship with God and with all humankind.

Through the centuries different forms of Christian spirituality have been practiced. Each has expressed a distinctive understanding of what it means to be united with the crucified Lord. Medieval piety included the devotional practice of meditating on the stations of the cross. Calvin described Christian life as self-denial and bearing the cross. Later pietists concentrated on the suffering and wounds of Jesus. Each Christian spirituality, at its best, has aimed at the transformation of human life from self-preoccupation to a new corporate identity through the power of God's self-giving and liberating love in Jesus Christ.

For many Christians earlier forms of spirituality have broken down. This breakdown is neither to be denied nor regretted. Becoming nostalgic about the forms of piety we have lost only compounds our problem. In Gutiérrez' words: "Not only is there a contemporary history and a contemporary Gospel; there is also a contemporary spiritual experience which cannot be overlooked. A spirituality means a reordering of the great axes of the Christian life in terms of this contemporary experience."[60] Like other aspects of the life of the church, the forms of spiritual life are historical and provisional. No less than doctrines or institutional structures, the spiritual life stands under the reforming authority of the Word of God as it addresses new situations. *Ecclesia semper reformanda* applies here as elsewhere.

The vacuum left by the breakdown of earlier forms of spirituality is being filled today in different ways. The charismatic movement has been a major force in the churches in recent years and has cultivated a particular kind of spirituality. Less influential but also significant has been the experimentation with the spiritual disciplines of the East. A critique of these movements is certainly legitimate to the extent that they focus on sensational phenomena, such as speaking in tongues, or confirm people in their apathy about social and political evils. But any critique of these movements would be blind if it failed to recognize the real crisis of spirituality in the churches to which these movements speak.

In the absence of a viable spirituality, many Christians simply take for granted the consumer way of life in a materialistic, technological society. The pattern of life becomes an endless and ultimately meaningless round of consuming and possessing things. This spirit of mastery and acquisition is necessarily aggressive because it never finds fulfillment. It drives toward the limitless exploitation of nature and of other human beings. Those who are captured by this spirit are themselves dehumanized as well as contributing to the dehumanization of others. As John Macquarrie writes: "In this very exploitation those who have such a mentality become themselves diminished in their humanity, for as they are dominated by the endless desire to have and to use and to consume they become less and less persons of freedom and dignity."[61]

We need a new spirituality that refuses to acquiesce to the spirit of conquest, possession, and consumption that characterizes the ethos of our society. We need a spirituality that frees us to work for the development of very different social attitudes and practices. We need a spirituality that connects us with the groaning of the whole creation for freedom. Gutiérrez is surely right: we need not less interest in the spiritual life but a radical transformation of it. We need a new spirituality that is inclusive rather than exclusive, active as well as receptive, oriented to the coming of God's kingdom of righteousness and freedom throughout the world. We need a spirituality of liberation that will open us increasingly to a life of solidarity with others, especially with the poor.

III

If there is a real crisis of Christian spirituality in many North American churches, the source of a new spirituality must be the biblical message of God's liberating activity and solidarity with the poor as this message is being heard today by the poor of the world. We must learn to hear the Bible not "from above," through the ears of those who are successful and comfortable, but "from below," through the ears of the unemployed, the uneducated, the exploited, and the despised.

Robert McAfee Brown gives a vivid illustration of hearing the Bible "from below" instead of "from above."

In a Central American country where poverty is rampant and dissenters are persecuted, a priest helps his people relate the biblical message to their situation. They note that this Sunday is September 12, the anniversary of the assassination of President Allende in Chile, and that it is also the Feast of the Holy Name of Mary. At first the people are unable to see any connection between Mary and such recent leaders of oppressed peoples as Allende, Mao and Martin Luther King. Then the priest reads the Song of Mary from Luke's Gospel. The text tells of Mary's surprise that God has chosen to identify with the weak and the poor. Mary sings: "[God] has scattered the proud in the imagination of their hearts, he has put down the mighty from their thrones, and exalted those of low degree; he has filled the hungry with good things, and the rich he has sent empty away" (Luke 1:51–53). After hearing this song, the people begin to contrast the Mary of the gospel with the Mary they know from going to the cathedral and from holy pictures. Unlike the glorious Mary of the cathedral and the holy pictures, the people conclude, the Mary of the gospel is one of us. In their imagination they now see her not as one who stands on the moon but in the dust and dirt with other poor people; she does not wear a crown but an old hat to shield her head from the sun; she has no rings and her hands are rough; she does not wear a purple and gold robe but old clothes. The people exclaim that Mary is more at home in the slum than in the cathedral.[62]

This story of the two Marys helps to clarify the differences between a spirituality of liberation and what Christians in North America ordinarily define as spirituality.

In the first place, the incident challenges the way we read the Bible. It brings home to us how selective our reading of the Bible is, how we automatically screen out passages and themes that would bring our social attitudes and practices under judgment. Our reading of the Song of Mary is so overlaid with either traditional Catholic Marian piety or the bourgeois Protestant cult of motherhood that we are insulated from the radical social implications of the passage. Johannes Metz speaks of the biblical narratives as containing a "dangerous and liberating memory."[63] He is thinking, of course, primarily of the passion narrative with its memory of the crucified Jesus and thus of God's utmost solidarity with the wretched of the world. But this dangerous memory is present throughout Scripture: in the exodus narrative, in the message of the prophets, in the Song of Mary, in Jesus' blessing of the poor, in his table fellowship with sinners, in his description of the goal of his ministry as the liberation of the oppressed. Thus one important question of authentic Christian spirituality is not simply *whether* we read the Bible but *how* we read the Bible. As we argued in Chapter 1, the

Bible must be read in a context of real solidarity with all people who are in bondage and groan for freedom. Third world Christians who are reading the Bible from below are finding in it an explosive message that the archbishops and the missionaries had not told them was there. Our reading of the Bible needs to be corrected and enriched by the perceptions of the poor.

Second, the story challenges our customary North American understanding of the experience of conversion and new birth. A typical conversion or new-birth experience as told by North American evangelists and revivalists is very different from the experience related in the story of the two Marys. Our new-birth stories concentrate on a prominent public figure who after a shoddy life of cheating and lying is finally "born again" and becomes a law-abiding citizen, or they tell of a born-again superstar whose experience shows that faith in Christ is compatible with or even a basis for success and stardom. By contrast, the story of the two Marys compels us to understand the meaning of rebirth in a very different way. The poor of the story do indeed experience a new birth; they come to a totally new understanding of God, of themselves, of God's will for humanity. Together they discover that Mary is one of them, the poor, and that God is deeply concerned about them, affirms them, identifies with them, wants them to be free. Their hearing and responding to the gospel message can instruct us. We have to learn from those who speak from below what the experience of new birth means for the poor and the oppressed. Otherwise our understanding of this experience will continue to be exceedingly narrow and superficial.

Third, the story implicitly challenges our practice of prayer. While the meaning of prayer is not explicitly discussed, it is certainly not far beneath the surface of the episode. The poor people of the story were no doubt taught from early childhood to say the Hail Mary, and they had probably repeated this prayer thousands of times. But after their discovery of the Mary of the gospel, the Hail Mary will mean something very different from what it meant when they knew only the Mary of the cathedral. The Hail Mary will now remind the one who prays of God's concern for righteousness on the earth, will sustain hope in God's promise, and will give assurance of God's solidarity in the midst of oppression. The Hail Mary will now create resistance to injustice rather than resignation to it. Those who pray from below can teach Catholics to pray the Hail Mary differently, and Protestants and Catholics to pray the Lord's Prayer differently. Christians pray, if they pray as Jesus taught his disciples, first and foremost for the hallowing of God's name, for the coming of God's kingdom, for the realization of God's will for righteousness, freedom, and peace on earth. Those who pray from below know that prayer is passionate and may take the form of a cry of godforsakenness (Mark 15:34). In memory of Jesus' cry of dereliction, praying in the name of Jesus means calling on God to let the righteousness of the kingdom be manifest over all the earth. Prayer is a form of resistance in a world marked by the idolatry of power and wealth instead of the hallowing of God's name, by the rule of violence instead of the dominion of forgiveness and friendship, by the will to control and exploit others instead of the will to self-expending love.[64]

Fourth, the story calls in question our common conceptions of the meaning of holiness and of the process of sanctification. When the poor thought of the holiness of the Mary of the cathedral and the holy pictures, holiness meant superiority, splendor, riches, and freedom from the grime and misery of this life. But the Mary of the gospel embodies a different kind of holiness. She is one of the poor in whom God's Holy Spirit is pleased to be present. Mary is full of grace because she is open to what God wants to do with and for the poor of the earth. If we listen to those who interpret from below the biblical description of the holiness of God and its call to the holy life, we will begin to understand holiness not in terms of freedom from vices frowned upon by conventional bourgeois morality but in terms of solidarity with people our society openly or secretly despises. It is the cross of Jesus which ultimately defines the meaning of God's holiness. Bearing the cross defines the process by which we are sanctified or made holy. We bear our cross as we enter into solidarity with the poor. Since Jesus has so freely identified himself with those in need, following him must take the form of concrete service to the hungry, thirsty, homeless, naked, sick, and imprisoned brothers and sisters of the crucified Lord (Matt. 25:31ff.). This is why Paul exhorts the Corinthians to express their solidarity with the poor of Jerusalem even as the Lord Jesus became poor for our sake (II Cor. 8:9). The holy church is the church in solidarity with the poor.[65]

IV

Our reflections to this point have made it clear that a spirituality of liberation will include many of the elements of earlier Christian spiritualities: Bible-reading, prayer, meditation, fellowship around Word and Sacrament, exercise of the gifts of the Spirit, service of the neighbor. But in the new spirituality these elements will acquire new meanings and uses because they will all be related to the praxis of Christian freedom in solidarity with the poor.

As we have seen, in a spirituality of liberation the Bible is read as the explosive story of God's liberation of people from all enslaving powers and of our partnership in this process.

Meditation becomes dangerous recollection and daring hope: the dangerous recollection of the cross of Christ which deepens our sensitivity to the cries of the oppressed, and the daring hope in, and vision of, the transformation of the whole creation by the love of God made known to us in the life, death, and resurrection of Christ.

Prayer includes praise and gratitude for God's unfathomable grace as well as confession of sin and a plea for forgiveness. But prayer also involves daring expostulation with God, asking when the righteousness of God will be manifest throughout the earth, children no longer abandoned to starvation, innocent people no longer murdered in the name of some ideology.

Fellowship around Word and Sacrament renews and clarifies the freedom for which Christ has set us free and gives us an anticipatory experience of the ultimate community of liberated creatures symbolized as the kingdom of God.

The gifts of the Spirit refer to all those resources of critical analysis, imagination, and compassion which Christians and others are given to contribute to the unfinished task of human liberation in all its dimensions.

The new spirituality of liberation is a political spirituality, but it is not the tailoring of Christian life to the measurements of particular political ideologies and programs. To speak of a political spirituality is to say that Christian devotion and commitment are not restricted to a private zone of existence but are directed toward new community, the full realization of human life in communion with God and with others.

The shift of Christian spirituality from preoccupation with the self to solidarity with the poor and the oppressed necessarily involves a new understanding of repentance, new birth, conversion, mortification, and commitment. In a spirituality of liberation the scope of these traditional terms is enlarged and their meaning is deepened.

Repentance involves renouncing not only our sins as individuals but also the evils of our society, which guards the privileges of some while holding others in bondage. Repentance includes the resolve to work for the transformation of political and economic structures that bring prosperity to our society by exploiting people of other lands.

Conversion means more than a turnaround in our private habits and activities. In its deepest sense, conversion means turning away from self-centeredness and turning to God who meets us in our neighbors. It means turning away from apathy, fear, and hopelessness—things which help to maintain the unjust conditions that hold our neighbors in bondage.

Mortification is far more than killing our inordinate personal desires and eliminating our petty vices. It means dying to a way of life based on the acquisitive mentality. It means dying to habits of consumption of the earth's resources that make life easier for a fraction of the world's population at the expense of the poor. It means ceasing to react in fear to every movement pressing for more just and equitable societies.

New birth symbolizes not only an event in personal history but also the beginning of new forms of society. Not only individuals but societies need to be open to basic changes if they are to be preparing the way for the kingdom of justice and freedom that God is bringing into being.

Christian commitment is neither devotion to an abstract Christ nor allegiance to a repressive moral code. It is trust in and loyalty to the crucified Christ whose emancipating Spirit guides the suffering creation toward the realization of "the glorious liberty of the children of God" (Rom. 8:21).

Authentic spiritual growth and the process of liberation are bound together as closely as the commandments to love God and to love our neighbors as ourselves. Rooted in the scriptural witness to God who takes up the cause of the oppressed, a spirituality of liberation motivates our participation in the struggle for social justice.

But it is equally true that liberation movements need the witness of Christian faith and life. In the first place, the experience of freedom as a gift, which is at the heart of a spirituality of liberation, points to the transcendent source of liberation and helps to guard the struggle for freedom against every absolutization of methods and achievements. Prayer, proclamation of the Word, and celebration of the Sacraments remind us that our hope is ultimately not in ourselves nor in our programs but in God.

Furthermore, we acknowledge in prayer and worship that we are sinners in need of God's forgiving and liberating grace. The enslaving forces of evil in the world are not only "out there" in oppressive social conditions but also at work in us.

Finally, a Christian spirituality perseveres in commitment to the process of liberation even in the face of disappointment and defeat. Celebration of the new freedom in Christ continually revives our passion for the fullness of liberty for the whole creation. Recognition of our solidarity with the poor of the earth is kept alive by trust in God who in Christ became one of the poor and godforsaken.

V

A spirituality of liberation will not emerge from mere theory. It will grow only in the actual practice of solidarity with the poor. A radical and costly conversion of our present attitudes and practices is required. In Gutiérrez' words: "A spirituality of liberation will center on a *conversion* to the neighbor, the oppressed person, the exploited social class, the despised race, the dominated country. Our conversion to the Lord implies this conversion to the neighbor."[66]

The call to a spirituality of liberation and to solidarity with the poor is a hard saying for middle-class North American Christians. How might we *begin* to respond to this call?

A first step would be for us North American Christians to achieve a critical awareness not only of the plight of poor people but also of our complicity in policies that exploit them. We must learn to listen. If we at least listen to what blacks, Latin Americans, and women are saying, there is a chance for the growth of a new critical awareness of ourselves and of our society. We should not underestimate the resistance to this arduous act of listening that will be encountered in ourselves and in the churches of suburban America. The judgment that is pronounced on the structures of political and economic power of which we are the beneficiaries is very severe. To listen to the charge that the comfortable way of life to which we have become accustomed is built upon the poverty of others is far from easy. It demands openness and honest self-examination as opposed to a spirit of defensiveness and self-deception. Thus the simple readiness to listen already constitutes a step in the direction of a new solidarity. Since prayer is always an exercise in listening as well as speaking, a community that has not forgotten how to pray will not have forgotten entirely how to listen. If our praying has disciplined us to genuine openness to God's will, it will also have prepared us for a new openness to the needs of our neighbors in this elementary sense of listening long and hard to their cries for justice and freedom.

Second, we have to become aware of our own bondage and differentiate it from the oppression experienced by the poor. "We are all oppressed," we may be tempted to say. In a certain sense this is true. All of us probably feel mistreated and victimized in some fashion at some time. But the systemic physical poverty and spiritual affliction experienced by millions of people in the world is not of the same order as the frustration, disappointment, and psychological distress experienced by relatively affluent people. Any attempt to blur this difference is a serious error. At the same time, North American Christians are in bondage and do need to be liberated. Our bondage is to the spirit of mastery, exploitation, and the consumer way of life. It is an illusion to think of ourselves as those who are free and of the poor of the earth as those who need to be rescued from their bondage to share in our freedom. This is arrogant and patronizing. True repentance would consist in the recognition of our own neediness. We are often accomplices of the "principalities and powers" of this world, and we too must cry out for God's liberating grace.

Third, we have to begin a new relationship with the poor and the oppressed in our own society and in our own community. This means, negatively, that we should not encourage romantic ideas of white, middle-class North American Christians leading the struggle for liberation in black communities or in third world countries. As Frederick Herzog has written, the struggle for liberation begins at home. "Liberation theology will be learned first of all in prison, in the migrant camp,

on a cotton field, in an Indian reservation or in the church
that will not ordain a woman as minister."[67] Talk of solidarity
with the poor must not be allowed to become mere rhetoric.
There must be concrete participation in a community struggling against oppression. The poor and oppressed are not
ideas but particular persons. If solidarity with the poor is to
be more than a mere idea or a patronizing gesture, it will
begin in relation to particular poor and neglected people in
our own society. Just as hearing God's Word and receiving
the bread and wine discipline our attention to the particularity of the gracious Lord who became poor for our sake,
so they discipline us to attend to the particularity of our
neighbors near and distant. If we are not engaged in the
struggle of the poor near us, we are unlikely ever to have any
real solidarity with the poor in distant lands.

Finally, solidarity with the poor is a meaningless phrase
apart from the beginnings of an actual transformation of our
style of life, as individuals and as a community of faith.
Affluent societies waste unconscionable amounts of natural
resources in their frenzy of self-indulgence and in their dark
fears which demand ever larger military machines to assuage.
Christian churches in these societies have not given witness
by the stewardship of their resources, nor have Christians, in
their own way of life, demonstrated an evangelical simplicity
of life-style. Only a way of life characterized by simplicity
and sacrifice could be a real basis for solidarity with the poor
and an authentic protest against material poverty. Gutiérrez
rightly insists that the call to Christian poverty should not be
understood as an idealization of material poverty. Christian
poverty is really an openness to God who though rich freely
became poor for the salvation of the world. Far from justify-
ing material poverty, this authorizes our protest against it. A
spirituality of liberation, based on the liberating, self-giving
love of God, would find its outward expression in a disciplined life of simplicity and in the readiness to risk ourselves
in acts of sacrificial love. It would involve protest, in concert
with the poor, against every way of life and every socioeco-

nomic system that enriches the few by impoverishing the many.

VI

In summary, there is indeed a great need for a spirituality of liberation. The need is present not only among Latin-American Christians struggling against poverty and the denial of human rights in their lands but also among Christians in North America. The old forms of spiritual life are dead, and the new ones that have appeared in our churches are often more alienating than life-transforming.

A spirituality of liberation, rooted in the biblical story of God's gift of freedom in Jesus Christ, can spring up and grow only in a practice of solidarity with the poor that "begins at home." The particular manifestations of this solidarity will differ according to the concrete situation. If they are not to become mere slogans, the call to a spirituality of liberation and the practice of solidarity with the poor will require costly changes of life-style for North American Christians. They will also require courage to oppose policies and systems that keep the poor in their poverty.

Resistance to basic changes in attitudes and ways of life is massive. Such resistance severely tests Christian hope. But Christian hope is not what the world calls optimism. It is a hope beyond hope, a hope in God who alone gives new life to the dead (Rom. 4:17). Christians remain faithful to God and to the cause of radical and inclusive liberation only if they bear witness to a power able to free people from the bondage of death. That is the subject of our final chapter.

Chapter 5

Liberation from the Bondage of Death

Any rethinking of basic Christian doctrines in the light of the gospel and in response to the human struggle for liberation will have to give special attention to the nature of Christian hope. What do Christians hope for in the face of death?

Much traditional Christian eschatology has been other-worldly and individualistic. It has offered to the suffering masses the consolation of heaven but has left them in inhuman conditions. It has promoted the belief that regardless of what happens in this life, there is another, eternal life after death in which justice will finally win out over the forces of evil and those now in bondage will finally be free. Such a doctrine empties the struggle for justice and freedom in history of all meaning. Otherworldly eschatology subverts the process of liberation.

This criticism of traditional Christian teaching about life after death has become almost commonplace in the modern period. It has been the premise of the Christian-Marxist dialogue in recent years. In this dialogue Christian theologians have readily admitted the distortions present in traditional Christian belief about life after death. At the same time, they have challenged Marxists to face squarely the reality of death and its erosive effects on commitment to the cause of universal justice and freedom. They have presented Christian hope not as an escape from history and liberation struggles but as a factor that mobilizes opposition to injustice and oppression and gives persons engaged in liberative activity both confidence and staying power.[68]

Traditional Christian eschatology, however, is not the only obstacle to a commitment to the process of liberation on the part of Christians. The beliefs of many people in Western society about death and life after death have been deeply influenced by the dominant technological ethos. There are images of death and immortality in American society today whose effect on engagement in the cause of liberation is no less negative than the escapism of "pie in the sky when you die" eschatology. A theology of liberation must be critical of the theological tradition, but it must also challenge the prevailing images of death in contemporary American culture.

Every culture has its characteristic images of death. The way a culture construes death and seeks to come to terms with it reveals what resources that culture possesses for full human life in freedom and solidarity. The symbols we use to speak of death, the framework of meaning within which we set it, the attitudes and dispositions we think are appropriate to it, will affect the way we order our life, set our priorities, and respond to the needs of other people.

I will argue that our dominant cultural images of death betray our fear of limitation, our inordinate self-regard, and our alienation from others. I will contend that, in contrast to the images of death in middle-class American culture, Christian faith sees death in a very different light, the light of the coming of God's kingdom of freedom made known in the crucified and risen Jesus.

I

If we ask what are the dominant images of death in American society today, I think there would be general agreement that at least three would have to be mentioned.

One powerful image of death in contemporary culture is

that of an enemy to be conquered by medical and technological mastery. This view has its roots in the Enlightenment. It is a secular version of the Christian promise of salvation from death. Not God but the scientific enterprise will finally defeat death, "the last enemy," and establish human immortality. This utopian expectation is given popular expression in a book by Alan Harrington, *The Immortalist.* According to Harrington, "Death is an imposition on the human race, and no longer acceptable. [Human beings have] all but lost [their] ability to accommodate [themselves] to personal extinction; [they] must now proceed physically to overcome it. In short, to kill death; to put an end to [human] mortality as a certain consequence of being born."[69] Totally opposed to all forms of acceptance of death, Harrington proposes that our society commit its resources to the conquest of death itself just as it has already virtually eliminated such diseases as smallpox. Our medical research and technology should be harnessed to the end of making human beings immortal, or at least of vastly increasing the span of human life. "Our new faith must accept as gospel that salvation belongs to medical engineering and nothing else." "Death," Harrington says flatly, "no longer fits into our plans."[70]

Harrington refuses to accept any distinction in principle between mortality as an aspect of our finite, contingent human nature and accidental, premature, or preventable death. All death is evil. Even so-called natural death at an advanced age is looked upon as an intolerable limit to human freedom and aspiration. This limit must now be shattered by human ingenuity.

Harrington's book is an extreme expression of uncritical faith in modern science and technology. There are no mysteries in the universe, only more or less difficult problems to be solved. The capacity of human beings to control nature and their own destiny is infinite. If we can travel to the moon, we can also make ourselves immortal. The exuberance of Harrington's presentation no doubt reflects the spirit of the 1960's: Utopia can be achieved through technology. Today we are more conscious of the limits of the growth that the natural resources of the world and the natural environment will permit. We are also more sober in our assessments of the impact of modern technology on the quality of human life. Nevertheless, the view of human mortality as an inadmissible fact that will eventually be conquered by science maintains its grip on the modern consciousness. In a recent book an ethicist argues that the ideal of immortality through modern medicine must be retained even if the ideal can never be realized.[71]

Of course, premature death and painful death are enemies of medicine. The protection of human life and the fight against avoidable death are ethical mandates. But when human mortality as such is considered an enemy to be conquered by science, an impulse to self-divinization, with all its destructive consequences, is at work. Several arguments against this impulse can be mounted.

First, the project of achieving immortality through the scientific conquest of the aging process assumes that the indefinite extension of life is an absolute good. This confuses quality with quantity. The idea that the human quest for fullness of life can automatically be satisfied by an indefinite extension of life is a tragic illusion. If the goodness of life is measured simply by the number of experiences we have, by the satisfaction of all conceivable desires, then the manufacture of immortality seems to make sense. If, however, the goodness of life is measured by a very different criterion, such as the love of God and of our neighbor, then the doubling or tripling of the human life span beyond its present seventy to eighty years fails to qualify as a high priority.

Second, the view of human mortality as an intrinsic evil usually involves an absolutization of the individual. The mutual dependence of the individual and society is disregarded. The individual raises the claim of his or her infinite value over against all social needs and values. When this claim is translated into practical proposals to achieve immortality through technology, the results are absurd. Cryonic societies offer the hope of deepfreezing at death until whatever caused the death of the individual can be cured. Such a hope is childishly romantic and thoroughly antisocial. Biologically and sociologically, the finitude and mortality of the individual represents a chance for the species and the social whole to be renewed. As we become increasingly aware of the population pressure and of our limited natural resources, the goal of the conquest of aging and death itself seems rooted more in anxiety than in genuine sensitivity to human suffering. In a society where many people are deprived of the most rudimentary medical care, and in a world where millions die yearly of malnutrition and disease, the argument to make prolongation of the life span a social priority in the United States and in other technologically advanced countries must be judged as egocentric and elitist.

Third, the ideology of immortality through science is simply an extension of the cultural ideals of affluent Western society. Among these ideals are the possession, control, and consumption of the world by the ego. All experiences of limitation and weakness are abhorred. Bigness is a virtue. Smallness is a vice. Strength is good. Weakness is bad. Life in the sense of continuous growth is unconditionally affirmed. Death as the ultimate event of passivity and powerlessness is thoroughly denied and concealed. The desire of omnipotence, of freedom from all experience of limitation and passivity, is deeply embedded in technocracy. This grasp for omnipotence is tragic and dehumanizing. At the level of the care of dying patients it finds expression in medical heroics that depersonalize and abuse the dying. At the level of social policy it takes the form of an idolatrous worship of unlimited expansion of a particular nation, culture, or way of life.

Reaction to the energy shortage is a case in point. Accustomed to virtually limitless consumption of energy, Americans now face the terror of the death of their profligate way of life. Despite the handwriting on the wall, the central article of American faith continues to be confidence in the ability of science and technology to save the people from all forms of social, cultural, and personal death.

II

A second widely held understanding of death in American society is that death is natural, a "fact of life" like being born, growing up, and growing old. The view of death as natural has been developed in recent years primarily in two contexts. One is the clinical context in which there is a strong pastoral concern to help the terminally ill rather than to abandon them out of fear. The other is the public-policy context in which the questions of the reasonable limits of the aspirations of medicine and of life-prolonging measures are raised.

The clinical concern is best represented by Elisabeth Kübler-Ross. Her popular and influential book, *On Death and Dying,* was written on the basis of years of experience of counseling dying patients. According to Kübler-Ross, our culture is thoroughly death-denying. This ethos of denial conspires to isolate the terminally ill. It prevents them from expressing their feelings, and thus abandons them, not necessarily in a physical but in an emotional sense, in their struggle to come to terms with their imminent death. Physicians, nurses, and chaplains, as well as the dying patients and the members of their families, form a silent conspiracy to deny what is actually happening. The whole structure of modern medical care is thus indicted with the charge of death-denial. Kübler-Ross suggests that this institutionalized denial of death sometimes takes a very aggressive form. She deplores the frantic mobilization of medical technology in the treatment of the dying to the point of disregarding them as human beings. She clearly repudiates the attitude toward death that sees it as an enemy to be resisted at all costs. She describes the terrible future toward which this attitude inexorably leads: "A look into the future shows us a society in which more and more people are 'kept alive' both with machines replacing vital organs and computers checking from time to time to see if some additional physiologic functionings have to be replaced by electronic equipment. Centers may be established in increasing numbers where all the technical data is collected and where a light may flash up when a patient expires in order to stop the equipment automatically."[72]

Kübler-Ross is best known for her description of the stages of the dying process. These include denial, anger, bargaining, depression, and final acceptance. These stages constitute a gradual, although unpredictable, process of working through the fear of death. The image of death which informs Kübler-Ross's analysis is death as the conclusion of a natural process, as a part of the eternal rhythm of nature. There is a mystical quality to her description of the naturalness of death. She compares the death of a human being to the light of a falling star, "one of the million lights in a vast sky that flares up for a moment only to disappear in the endless night forever." Despite our brief life span, our unique biography is somehow woven into the fabric of human history and thus has its lasting significance.

Of course, in speaking of death as natural, Kübler-Ross does not propose that we dismantle our hospitals and discontinue all advanced medical procedures. Rather, her point is that all of our medical know-how should be employed within the framework of a realistic acknowledgment of the limited life span of a human being and of the inherent limitations of medical treatment. Death is not an enemy to be conquered by medical technology, but an inherent part of the natural growth process. Human life has a beginning and an end. Given the proper caring environment, most people will finally accept death in peace.

Kübler-Ross's contribution has been considerable. She has courageously resisted the ideological warfare against death as such and its demonic elements. She has shown that there is a need and an obligation to continue to care for the dying even when cure is no longer possible.

Nevertheless, questions must be raised about her description of death as a natural event. One question concerns her description of acceptance as the goal of the dying process. Roy Branson has argued that the final stage of acceptance in Kübler-Ross's analysis of the stages of dying is more prescriptive than descriptive.[73] Acceptance of death thus becomes a norm or expectation in our dealings with the dying. This is problematic. If acceptance of death is a standard that we subtly impose upon those with whom we company in their dying, we cut ourselves off from them to the extent that they continue to express their passion for life. The anguish experienced by Jesus in his dying, in contrast to Socrates' serene acceptance, exposes the dimension of darkness in death. According to the Gospel of Mark, the final word of Jesus was the question why God had abandoned him (Mark 15:34). This cry for God's kingdom to be manifest on the earth stands in opposition to every acceptance of death that amounts to resignation to suffering and injustice in an estranged world.

The ambiguity present in the description of death as natural and in the therapy of acceptance has a wider, sociopolitical importance. When is natural death merely socially contrived death? How is acceptance of death to be distinguished from hopeless resignation to what is thought to be the iron law of the universe? Surely every death cannot be appropriately described as natural and acceptable. Otherwise no death would be unjust, premature, outrageous. Death in all its forms would simply be the fate to which we must resign ourselves. Acceptance of death in this sense would be an ideology as dehumanizing as the pretentious program to conquer all death through medical science and technology. Martin Luther King and Stephen Biko did not die natural deaths. Millions of other victims of hatred and oppression did not die natural deaths.

What is meant by natural death must be defined more carefully. This is attempted in recent literature exploring the significance for public policy of a concept of natural death. According to Daniel Callahan, a concept of natural death is needed in modern society in order to set reasonable limits to the aspirations of medical science and to give moral guidance regarding our obligations to the dying.[74] Broadly speaking, natural death is defined as death that does not either come prematurely or involve intolerable pain. It is death that comes as a result of the weakness of old age. This "modern" definition of natural death is not far from the Old Testament description of the death of the patriarchs after a long and full life (Gen. 15:15; Judg. 8:32; Job 42:17; etc.). According to this strand of the Old Testament, death is not necessarily a violent, untimely, or meaningless end. It might be experienced as the natural conclusion of life. This way of speaking of death as natural is more like an ideal, i.e., of what death might be, than a description of death as it is actually experienced. The importance of understanding death as something that is not necessarily evil but that might be experienced as natural (and in some cases is so experienced) is hard to overestimate in a society saturated with the abhorrence of all limits.

Nevertheless, the tension between what death might be and what it is must not be ignored. For Christian faith the concept of natural death must be qualified in at least two respects. One qualification is that human beings are "liberated for natural death" by faith in the gracious God who is revealed decisively in Jesus Christ.[75] The attainment of old age does not guarantee that a person is able to accept the life that is now coming to an end. God's radical acceptance of us by grace is the basis of our acceptance of our life with its beginning and its end as natural. The other necessary qualification is that when natural death means what death might be, it is "charged with social-critical power."[76] Precisely because of our commitment to and passion for the fullness of life as intended by God, we must fight against all socially contrived premature and violent death. The concept of natural death, properly understood, does not encourage apathy and resignation but represents a commitment to fullness of life for all people. We betray our lack of commitment to freedom for others when we demand that we be allowed to die a natural death but remain apathetic about the socially manufactured deaths of the poor and wretched of the earth.

III

The most recent work of Kübler-Ross has been with people who have had near-death experiences or who have actually been declared clinically dead and then have been revived. On the basis of her research, she claims that she now believes in a life after death, "beyond the shadow of a doubt." There has been an outpouring of articles and books on this topic, and at least one has even made the best-seller list. Here we encounter a third image of death in American society today. Death is seen as the release of the immortal soul from the earthly body. This is by no means a new understanding of death. Nevertheless, it has attracted wide interest because of the scientific credentials with which it is now advanced.

Kübler-Ross's own research in this area has yet to be published. However, she has spoken approvingly of a recent book by Raymond Moody, *Life After Life.* On the basis of some fifty cases of near-death and clinical-death experiences, Moody argues that there is evidence (not yet proof) of the reality of life after death. There were a number of common elements in the experiences reported by Moody. Persons who were interviewed mentioned floating out of the physical body and observing from a short distance the frantic efforts of the medical team to revive the corpse on the bed; feeling very peaceful; meeting loved ones who had died before them; being confronted by a religious figure, a "being of light," who acted as companion and interpreter of the events of their past life; wishing they could remain in their new condition but finding themselves once again reunited with their earthly body. Those who have had such experiences have met with skepticism or ridicule when they have tried to relate to others what had happened to them. Still, these experiences have had a deep impact on their subsequent life and on their view of death.

We will not go into Moody's data and findings in any detail. A few quotations from persons interviewed by him will suffice to give the essence of the understanding of death produced by these experiences. According to one person: "After you've once had the experience that I had, you know in your heart that there's no such thing as death. You just graduate from one thing to another—like from grammar school to high school to college." Another person stated: "Life is like imprisonment. In this state, we just can't understand what prisons these bodies are. Death is such a release —like an escape from prison. That's the best thing I can think of to compare it to.'"" Thus for many people who have had out-of-the-body experiences, death is symbolized not as an enemy to be unconditionally resisted, nor as an inescapable part of the eternal rhythm of nature, but as an event of liberation, the release of the immortal soul from the body and its graduation to a higher state of existence.

There are dangers in a doctrine of immortality, whether it be of the classical Platonic type or of the newer quasi-scientific type. The most important of these dangers is the tendency to disparage bodily existence and to reduce life in this world to a second-rate value at best. The doctrine of the immortality of the soul implies a fundamental dualism. Life is separated into discrete spheres of the spiritual and the physical. There is a breakdown of passionate commitment to life and love in the body. Interest in and love for other people and this world dwindle, for these belong, as our bodies belong, to the physical domain. The will to love cannot long survive when the fear of death has been overcome by some form of dualistic belief. When the immortality of the soul is the content of our hope in the face of death, hope in the biblical sense is drastically abridged. It is cut down to survival of the self isolated from everyone and everything save perhaps a narrow circle of family and friends.

Nevertheless, there is an important element of truth in

these intimations of immortality reported by Moody and others. It is at least dimly recognized that a way of life based on the possession and consumption of things, on the satisfaction and security offered by an abundance of plastic and electronic gadgets, has no lasting value. Our possessive and wasteful way of life is a way of death. It has no future. But the doctrine of the immortality of the soul is an illusory solution to a real problem. What we reach out for in our disenchantment with a narcissistic and materialistic way of life is not escape from this world but its transformation, not the abandonment of the body but its resurrection, not the preservation of our exclusive communities but the creation of a new, inclusive community.

IV

I said at the outset that Christian faith looks at death in the light of God's coming kingdom decisively revealed in Jesus the crucified Lord and his liberating Spirit, It is the task of Christian theology to articulate this conviction in critical dialogue with the understandings of death dominant in contemporary culture. Within the limits of this chapter only a sketch of this project can be offered.

1. Over against the fear of death that manifests itself in the spirit of technological omnipotence stands the Christian affirmation of the creative love of God.

God is creator. Human beings are creatures. As creatures we are spatially and temporally limited. We are finite and mortal. We are historically and culturally conditioned. These are the limits within which created human freedom must be actualized. According to the biblical understanding, human finitude is not something intrinsically evil. The world that God created is good, and this includes the fact that each human life has a beginning and an end. Temporal limitation is a condition of the possibility of authentic human freedom and moral growth. If human life were temporally infinite, it would lack moral seriousness. We pray to God to teach us to number our days because the days we have for the acquisition of wisdom and for spending ourselves in the love and service of God and of our fellow creatures are not limitless. If our time stretched out infinitely, no particular time would ever be decisive, urgent, or precious. If we follow the guidance of the biblical witness, we will not view our finitude and mortality as intrinsically evil but as the condition of the possibility of learning to love in freedom.

One of the problems in understanding the meaning of human creatureliness is that it has too often been presented as the corollary of absolute divine power. According to this view, the divine monarch wanted no competitors in the created order. Omnipotence and absolute freedom were reserved for God alone. Hence human life was shackled with all sorts of limitations and restrictions. The motivating dynamic of modern atheism is its protest against this monarchic conception of the creator God in the name of human freedom and dignity.

But such an understanding of God as creator and human beings as creatures is a gross distortion of the biblical view. Creation is not an arbitrary display of omnipotence. If it were, then the critics of Christian faith in God would be right in charging that God is simply the oppressive power of Caesar writ infinitely large. Instead, creation is a divine risk. In creating another and entering into relationship with this other, God becomes vulnerable. The act of creation is an act of free self-limitation by God. God freely accepts limitation in order to love.[78]

Such an understanding of the creative love of God is of course shaped by the definitive expression of God's freedom to love in Jesus Christ. The creator and the redeemer are not two gods but one and the same. In the light of the life, death, and resurrection of Jesus, the confession of God as creator and of ourselves as creatures gains an entirely new meaning. We are limited as creatures not in order to vindicate the omnipotence of God but in order to make authentic love and community possible. For there is no open relationship with others where there is no self-limitation. Our willingness to accept limitation and vulnerability for the sake of love is a reflection of the free self-limitation of God in creation.

Within this perspective the effort to immortalize ourselves through medical technology is exposed as an attack on love rather than the affirmation of life and community which it purports to be. Can anyone doubt at whose expense the program of immortality through medical science would be bought? The cost would obviously be paid finally by the poor, hungry, and helpless people of the world who do not have the luxury of deciding whether it might be a fine thing to increase the human life span to one hundred years or more. The goal of indefinite self-preservation is surely the death of love in a world filled with socially manufactured misery.

A recognition of limits is essential if human beings are to live in fruitful freedom with and for each other as God intends. When the project of self-realization knows no boundaries, violence is done to others and to ourselves. Self-restraint and self-discipline, exercised both at personal and social levels, are qualities of an extraordinary freedom. This different freedom is ultimately rooted in the free self-limitation of God.

2. Over against every indiscriminate description of death as natural which fosters apathy and hopelessness stands the Christian affirmation of the suffering love of God.

We have already indicated that the idea of natural death represents at least one strand of the biblical understanding of death. In our modern technological society it is very important that this biblical strand be retrieved. To speak of death as natural is, in the modern context, to oppose the drive for human control of nature which recognizes no limits. Speaking of death as natural acts as a check on that will to perpetuate the self which disregards the question of the quality of life for all people and concentrates on the mere quantitative extension of life for a few. Christian faith recognizes the legitimacy of the concept of natural death.

Nevertheless, the description of death as part of the rhythm of nature is ideological when it serves to cover up the connection between sin, evil, and death in human existence. Death as it is actually experienced and known in history is burdened with guilt, violence, and terror. This is why the apostle Paul can speak of death as the "wages of sin" (Rom. 6:23). Of course, sin is not the cause of human mortality as such, as much traditional Christian theology has taught. Rather, death is the wages of sin in the sense that it exposes the drive toward self-centered existence which rules our individual life and our social orders. We fear death because it ruthlessly exposes the direction of our life toward relationlessness.[79] Death as the natural end of life is deeply hidden beneath the fearful, judgmental, violent form that it characteristically assumes in a sinful world. Hence those who speak of death as enemy and curse are closer to the truth of actual human experience than those who try to beautify death by calling it friend or brother.

On the social level, the understanding of death as natural may gloss over the extent to which death is a means of social and political control. When economic systems function to perpetuate the chasm between the rich and the poor, when political systems maintain their power by a reign of violence and murder, death is not natural. It is the instrument of human sin, a social contrivance that enables the rich and powerful to defy the natural as created by God. The concept of natural death is theologically legitimate only when it is "charged with social-critical power" rather than being part of an ideology that justifies socially manufactured misery and death.

The reign of unnatural death in human history makes us apathetic and hopeless. The Christian proclamation of the suffering love of God struggles against this tendency. It has often been said that human beings make their gods in their own image. There is truth in this claim. Yet it is also important to recognize that our human living and dying are shaped by the images of God that we hold. If as some ancient Greek philosophers described the deity, God is beyond all passion, all change, all caring or loving or suffering, then to be godlike is to be beyond all passion for life, all protest against injustice, all sensitivity to those in bondage. Apathy, withdrawal, and cynical indifference become a way of life and a way of death for those who think of the freedom of God as the freedom of indifference. In this view of God the highest wisdom of life and death is to extinguish all passion, all hope, all love.

The God of the biblical witness is very different. As Abraham Heschel wrote, the God of the Bible is a God of pathos.[80] God cares for his people, is affected by their actions and their sufferings, is enraged at injustice and the abuse of the poor. The God of Israel is not an impassive, absolute being but a relational God who not only acts but also suffers with his people.

The person who lives in covenant with this passionate God cannot become apathetic. Such a person lives sympathetically, compassionately, by sharing in the pathos of God and in the suffering of fellow creatures caused by injustice and exploitation.[81]

The Christian community sees the passion of God decisively revealed in the ministry and death of Jesus. He made no attempt to evade the dark and negative dimensions of human existence. In his companying with sinners, the demon-possessed, and the incurably ill, and conclusively in his own passion and death, Jesus embodied the suffering love of God for all. In mediating the forgiving love of God, he removed the sting of death, the obsession with our own self which causes us to disregard others and the coming kingdom of God. In the passion and death of Jesus, God suffered with all who suffer by reason of neglect, violence, and hate. Only in this way can and does God help us. To participate in the Spirit of the crucified and risen Jesus is to receive the forgiveness of God through him and to share in his passion for a free and transformed world.

3. Over against the bifurcation of life so often associated with belief in the immortality of the soul stands Christian

hope in the victorious love of God who raised Jesus from the dead.

The doctrines of immortality and of life after death have been subjected to sharp pyschological and sociological criticisms. Psychologically, the idea of immortality has been attacked as providing religious sanction to the human illusions of omnipotence and deathlessness. Sociologically, it has been accused of offering postmortem compensation to those who are oppressed and exploited in this world.

Christian hope does not need to be afraid of these criticisms. Nor does it rest on philosophical proofs or scientific evidence, if there be such, of the survival of the soul beyond death. In the light of Jesus Christ, Christians believe in God who raises the dead. There are at least two important differences between belief in the immortality of the soul and faith in God whose triumphant love is symbolized by the term "resurrection." First, resurrection is a gracious act of God. The word *athanasia,* "immortality," appears in only two passages in the New Testament. In I Tim. 6:16 immortality is ascribed not to human beings but to God. Thus immortality is not something human beings have in themselves; it is a free gift from the one who alone is immortal. This is the point of I Cor. 15:53f., where Paul says that by the resurrection of the dead we who are mortal will be clothed with immortality. Second, the resurrection of the body points to life in community as the meaning of eternal life. Hope in the resurrection of the dead envisions the goal of human life not as the survival of the self in isolation but as the completion of perfect community with God and with others.

Belief in God who raised the crucified Jesus and who has thereby shown us the "first fruits" of the new kingdom of righteousness, freedom, and love, keeps us loyal to the earth. As Dietrich Bonhoeffer wrote: "It is only when one loves life and the earth so much that without them everything seems to be over that one may believe in the resurrection and a new world."[82]

Christians know a new freedom in Christ. They are moved

by his liberating Spirit. But they are not yet entirely free, nor is the creation as a whole liberated from its bondage. While we are participating now in the freedom, joy, and peace of the life-giving Spirit of God, the freedom we experience is anticipatory. We continue to yearn together with the whole groaning creation for that total transformation of our lives called by faith the resurrection of the body, and for that total transformation of the world and all its relationships called by faith the kingdom of God. In the New Testament, it is especially Paul who reminds Christian believers that the new life of the Spirit of freedom and sacrificial service that is at work among them has not yet reached its goal. There is an eschatological reservation in the New Testament. Celebration of the new freedom is therefore anticipatory in nature. The resurrection of the body is still something hoped for and not an accomplished fact. Thus Christians must wait, in solidarity with the creation in travail, for the consummation of God's liberating activity. Evil and death continue to exercise power in the world even though their ultimate destruction is now sure. In the time before the completion of God's kingdom, Christians anticipate the final triumph of God's love by their Spirit-given freedom to enter into solidarity with the hungry, the thirsty, the stranger, the naked, the sick, the imprisoned (Matt. 25:31ff.).

Christian hope differs radically from humanistic hope in a better future because it knows a power that is stronger than death. Humanistic hopes, whether Marxist or bourgeois, look to a future in history that will justify all the misery of history. The seeds of despair are present in these hopes. Why should one suffer and sacrifice for a golden age in the distant future when one will have been swallowed by death long before the awaited eschaton? With this question the dominion of death insinuates itself into our hope. We are tamed to adjust to the way things are. We are domesticated and learn to get used to evil, suffering, and death, which once aroused our protest. This is the story of many revolutions in human history. They have eventually been conquered by the counterrevolution of death and the hopelessness and indifference that fear of it breeds.

Hope in God and the coming kingdom is different from both the individualistic reduction of hope to the survival of the self and from the vision of a distant society in which humanity finally comes to full self-realization. In short, Christian hope is different from bourgeois individualism and from Marxist utopianism. Christian hope is hope for the whole creation. It includes the dead as well as the living. God's lordship of self-giving love will reign throughout the creation. Paul assures the anxious Christians of Thessalonica that when the Lord comes the living will not have any advantage over the dead (I Thess. 4:15). In this way Paul rejects the idea that human beings living now are only stepping stones to a future fulfillment to be enjoyed by others. By our life in the Spirit who brings freedom and solidarity with the oppressed we participate in a provisional way in God's kingdom now. Neither the living nor the dead have the advantage, since nothing can separate us from the love of God in Christ Jesus (Rom. 8:38f.). With this assurance Christians invest themselves freely in the service of others. Trusting in the victorious love of God who raised Jesus from the dead and sent his Spirit as the "first fruits" of the coming kingdom, Christians are liberated from the bondage of death and for the life of service and solidarity.

Twisted ideas of God and eternal life go hand in hand with social injustice and indifference to the suffering of others. Conversely, the understanding of God as triune is the basis both of Christian life in solidarity with the whole enslaved creation and of inclusive Christian hope. As was emphasized in Chapter 3, the doctrine of the Trinity speaks of the mystery of God as a history of self-expending, community-forming love. God is no solitary monad whose life is closed to others. God's being is in community, and God creates community. If the life of the triune God is defined by free self-giving love, privatism has no place in Christian hope. Our destiny as persons and the completion of God's purposes for the entire creation are indivisible. This is not to say that individuals are unimportant in the purpose of God. Rather, it is to recognize that we become fully personal only in relationship. The completion of our lives as persons involves a depth of fellowship with God and with others of which we have now only a foretaste. Opposition between the quest for personal fulfillment and concern for the liberation of all creation is alien to authentic Christian hope. The goal of the struggle for liberation is not the Western ideal of self-realization. Nor is it the Eastern ideal of undifferentiated unity. It is the joyful participation of God's liberated creatures in the inexhaustibly rich communion of the eternal life of God.[83]

To affirm the resurrection of the dead is to trust in the triumph of the love of the triune God. It is to confess that God's way of self-expending love, which accepts the risk of suffering in resistance to the powers of self-assertion, injustice, and socially manufactured misery and death, represents an altogether different freedom, a freedom for others that is stronger than death.

Conclusion

In the preceding pages I have tried to show both the importance and the limits of reinterpreting the Christian message for our time as God's liberating activity in which we are called to take part. The theology of liberation is a challenge to Christians everywhere. It should be neither ignored nor dismissed as a passing theological fad. The ecumenical church should welcome this challenge to move toward a deeper understanding of and commitment to the gospel of freedom.

I have reformulated several basic Christian doctrines and have lifted up the theme of liberation in each. Two important conclusions may be drawn from this study. One is that the Christian doctrinal heritage must itself be liberated if it is genuinely to serve the liberating gospel. The doctrine of Scripture must be freed from theories and presuppositions that prevent Scripture from functioning as liberating word. The doctrine of Jesus the Christ must be freed both from a docetic otherworldliness and from ideological portrayals of Jesus as the hero of a particular social movement. The liberating activity of Jesus is different. The classical doctrine of God needs to be liberated from a conceptuality that is unable to express the profound relationship between the activity of the triune God and the struggles and sufferings of the creation groaning in bondage and yearning to be free. The doctrine of the spiritual life needs to be liberated from self-preoccupation, and the doctrine of eternal life needs to be freed from its cultural captivities. When Christian doctrines are rightly interpreted, they bear witness to the gospel of freedom. Their intent is to speak of God not as the enemy but as the foundation of authentic human freedom. The freedom of God made known in the crucified and risen Lord is the creative source of all freedom and the paradigm by which every expression of freedom is ultimately to be measured. God actualizes his freedom as freedom for others, as the freedom for partnership, as the freedom to love. Participation in this divine way of being free is the foundation and goal of human life in freedom.

Much of our theology and piety is enslaved to individualism and privatism. I have emphasized that the liberating power of the gospel has both personal and sociopolitical dimensions. These dimensions should not be set over against each other. The call to faith in the gracious God and the call to freedom from all forms of bondage go hand in hand. The forgiveness of God mediated by Christ, his gracious acceptance of sinners, results in a new birth of freedom. Persons are released from their bondage to self-centeredness, self-righteousness, self-hatred, hopelessness, and indifference. They are enabled to find in God the only proper object of trust and unconditional loyalty. But this freedom which we receive as a gift is also our task. We are called to practice and promote the new freedom in Christ in every domain of life. True liberation is comprehensive. It is political, cultural, and ecological as well as personal.

The other important conclusion of our study is that the Christian understanding of freedom, when faithful to the gospel, is provocatively different. It is not merely an echo of whatever goes under the name of liberation or freedom in a particular culture or political movement. If we have emphasized that basic Christian doctrines come alive in a new way when interpreted in relation to real human bondage and liberation, we have also emphasized that the understanding of freedom undergoes transformation as it is shaped by the Christian gospel and by the central doctrines of the faith. As revealed in Jesus Christ, the freedom of God is the freedom of a judging grace and a gracious judgment, the freedom to love, the freedom for others, and especially the freedom of solidarity with the despised, the afflicted, the poor, and the godforsaken. What the churches in North America have to hear more plainly and bear witness to in word and deed is that Christian freedom is not self-centered. It certainly does not consist in the possession and consumption of things or in the manipulation and control of others. Authentic Christian freedom corresponds to the freedom of the God of the gospel. This new freedom will express itself today in joyful service of God and of our fellow creatures, in self-restraint and self-limitation in the use of natural resources, in the will to inclusive community as opposed to the will to power over others manifest in all forms of sexism, racism, and class domination, in respect for and celebration of the diversity of God's creatures, in the spirit of solidarity with the poor of the earth and with all who are oppressed and who cry out for freedom.

I have insisted that the middle-class church in North America has much to learn from the theologies of liberation. At the same time I have pointed out, as liberation theologians themselves have often done, the dangers of misunderstanding the proclamation of God's liberating activity. There is the temptation to identify political programs with the kingdom of God and to assume human liberation can be accomplished entirely by social or political change; there is the tendency to fall into a simplistic dualism of oppressed and oppressors; there is the danger of a spirit of self-righteousness and legalism in working for a more just and equitable social order; there is the inclination to discount the theological tradition as irrelevant to present revolutionary praxis; there is the possibility of subtly transforming the Christian message of salvation by grace through faith into a religion of works; there is the danger of emphasizing only the bright symbols of exodus, resurrection, and hope while forgetting the dark symbols of journey through the wilderness, crucifixion, and costly discipleship. These dangers are real and cannot be dismissed as predictable objections of the defenders of the status quo. Despite these dangers, or rather precisely because of them, the response of the whole church should be to work toward a more adequate, more faithful understanding and practice of the freedom for which Christ has set us free. If there is need to engage in criticism of recent theologies of liberation, let this not be done in an attitude of complacency. Rather let the whole church cultivate a theology and practice of Christian freedom that is both passionate and critical, both imaginative and responsible, both grounded in the witness of Scripture and involved in the struggles and sufferings of the poor and the oppressed.

These remarks bring us full circle to our point of departure. What has been offered here is only an introduction. We have engaged in experimental theology, a theology *in via,* on the way toward a more adequate understanding of the freedom of God and of the new human freedom rooted in faith in God. The theology of the future will have to be a genuinely open ecumenical venture. The age of exporting theology from Europe and the United States to the third world of Latin America, Africa, and Asia is over. It is long past time for the churches in societies obsessed with a self-centered consumer way of life to listen carefully and to respond faithfully to the voices of the poor and to the cries of people whose fundamental human rights are systematically violated. We are called, both as individuals and as a community, to repent and to turn in a new direction. We are summoned to bear witness, in our proclamation and practice, to the gospel of Jesus Christ, to the good news of God's freedom for the world and of his call to freedom.

Notes

1. Jürgen Moltmann, *Religion, Revolution, and the Future,* tr. by M. Douglas Meeks (Charles Scribner's Sons, 1969), p. 67.

2. Gustavo Gutiérrez, *A Theology of Liberation,* tr. by Caridad Inda and John Eagleson (Orbis Books, 1973), p. 308.

3. Gordon D. Kaufman, "What Shall We Do with the Bible?" *Interpretation,* Vol. XXV, No. 1 (Jan. 1971), pp. 95–112.

4. Cf. Heinrich Heppe, *Reformed Dogmatics,* tr. by G. T. Thomson (London: George Allen & Unwin, 1950).

5. Charles Hodge, *Systematic Theology* (1871–72; Wm. B. Eerdmans Publishing Co., 1960), Vol. I, p. 152.

6. Hans Frei, *The Eclipse of Biblical Narrative* (Yale University Press, 1974).

7. Karl Barth, "The Strange New World Within the Bible," in *The Word of God and the Word of Man,* tr. by Douglas Horton (Harper & Brothers, Harper Torchbooks, 1957), pp. 28–50.

8. Martin Luther, Preface to the Epistles of St. James and St. Jude (1522), quoted by Karl Barth, *Church Dogmatics,* Vol. I, Part 2, ed. by G. W. Bromiley and T. F. Torrance (Edinburgh: T. & T. Clark, 1956), p. 478.

9. Barth, *Church Dogmatics,* Vol. I, Part 2, p. 463.

10. Barth, *Church Dogmatics*, Vol. IV, Part 3, Second Half, pp. 647–680.

11. *The Book of Confessions*, 2d ed. (The Office of The General Assembly of The United Presbyterian Church in the United States of America, 1970), paragraphs 9.06 and 9.29.

12. Jürgen Moltmann, *Theology of Hope*, tr. by James W. Leitch (Harper & Row, 1967), p. 21.

13. Cf. Barth, *Church Dogmatics*, Vol. I, Part 2, pp. 661–695.

14. Cf. Walter Kreck, *Grundfragen der Dogmatik* (Munich: Chr. Kaiser, 1970), pp. 44ff.

15. See Rudolf Bultmann, *Existence and Faith: Shorter Writings of Rudolf Bultmann*, tr. and ed. by Schubert M. Ogden (Meridian Books, 1960), esp. pp. 294–295.

16. Krister Stendahl, *The Bible and the Role of Women: A Case Study in Hermeneutics* (Fortress Press, Facet Books, 1966), pp. 32ff. Cf. also Letty M. Russell, *Human Liberation in a Feminist Perspective: A Theology* (Westminster Press, 1974), pp. 78–89.

17. Cf. David H. Kelsey, *The Uses of Scripture in Recent Theology* (Fortress Press, 1975), pp. 207–216.

18. Cf. Eugene TeSelle, *Christ in Context* (Fortress Press, 1975), p. xi.

19. Cf. José Miguez-Bonino, *Doing Theology in a Revolutionary Situation* (Fortress Press, 1975).

20. Hans Küng, *On Being a Christian*, tr. by Edward Quinn (Doubleday & Co., 1976), p. 123.

21. See James Cone, *A Black Theology of Liberation* (J. B. Lippincott Co., 1970), pp. 197–227; Gustavo Gutiérrez, *A Theology of Liberation*, pp. 168–178; Frederick Herzog, *Liberation Theology* (Seabury Press, 1972), pp. 45–116; Peter C. Hodgson, *New Birth of Freedom* (Fortress Press, 1976), pp. 208–264.

22. Hans Frei, *The Identity of Jesus Christ* (Fortress Press, 1975), p. 136.

23. Cf. Hans Kessler, *Erlösung als Befreiung* (Düsseldorf: Patmos Verlag, 1972), pp. 43–60.

24. Anselm of Canterbury, *Cur Deus Homo,* especially II, 17.

25. Søren Kierkegaard, *Philosophical Fragments,* tr. by David F. Swenson, tr. rev. by Howard V. Hong (Princeton University Press, 1962), p. 87.

26. See Günther Bornkamm, tr. by Irene and Fraser McLuskey with James M. Robinson, *Jesus of Nazareth* (Harper & Brothers, 1960), pp. 53–143; Küng, *On Being a Christian,* pp. 145–462.

27. Walter Kasper, *Jesus the Christ* (Paulist Press, 1976), p. 245.

28. Eberhard Jüngel, *Gott als Geheimnis der Welt* (Tübingen: J. C. B. Mohr, 1977), pp. 422f.

29. George Hendry, *The Gospel of the Incarnation* (Westminster Press, 1958), p. 103. Bracketed words in this and other quotations are slight changes made in order to employ inclusive language.

30. Cone, *A Black Theology of Liberation,* pp. 210–211.

31. Jürgen Moltmann, *The Church in the Power of the Spirit* (Harper & Row, 1977), p. 121.

32. Cf. Douglas John Hall, *Lighten Our Darkness: Toward an Indigenous Theology of the Cross* (Westminster Press, 1976).

33. Moltmann, *The Church in the Power of the Spirit,* p. 262.

34. Hodgson, *New Birth of Freedom,* p. 238.

35. Paul Lehmann, *The Transfiguration of Politics* (Harper & Row, 1975), pp. 271ff.

36. Russell, *Human Liberation in a Feminist Perspective— A Theology,* p. 168.

· 37. John Calvin, *Institutes of the Christian Religion,* Vol. I, ed. by John T. McNeill, The Library of Christian Classics, Vol. XX (Westminster Press, 1960), p. 122.

38. Jürgen Moltmann, "The Trinitarian History of God," *Theology,* Vol. LXXVIII, No. 666 (Dec. 1975), p. 632.

39. Dietrich Bonhoeffer, *Letters and Papers from Prison,* ed. by Eberhard Bethge (Macmillan Co., 1972), p. 286.

40. Jüngel, *Gott als Geheimnis der Welt*, p. 449.

41. Jürgen Moltmann, *The Crucified God*, tr. by R. A. Wilson and John Bowden (Harper & Row, 1974), p. 252.

42. H. Richard Niebuhr, *The Meaning of Revelation* (Macmillan Co., 1941), p. 187.

43. Arthur C. McGill, *Suffering: A Test of Theological Method* (Westminster Press, Geneva Press Book, 1968), pp. 66–67.

44. Karl Barth, *Dogmatics in Outline*, tr. by G. T. Thomson, (London: SCM Press, 1949), p. 48.

45. McGill, *Suffering*, p. 68.

46. Jan Milič Lochman, "The Trinity and Human Life," *Theology*, Vol. LXXVIII, No. 658 (April, 1975), p. 180.

47. John Macmurray, *Persons in Relation* (London: Faber & Faber, 1961), p. 61.

48. Juan Luis Segundo, *Our Idea of God*, tr. by John Drury (Orbis Books, 1974), pp. 81, 66.

49. Eberhard Jüngel, *The Doctrine of the Trinity* (Wm. B. Eerdmans Publishing Co., 1977), p. 100.

50. Cf. Karl Rahner, *The Trinity*, tr. by Joseph Donceel (Herder & Herder, 1970), pp. 21–22.

51. Moltmann, *The Church in the Power of the Spirit*, pp. 62–63.

52. Segundo, *Our Idea of God*, p. 102.

53. Joseph A. Bracken, *What Are They Saying About the Trinity?* (Paulist Press, 1979), p. 63.

54. An earlier version of this chapter appeared in *A Christian Declaration on Human Rights*, ed. by Allen O. Miller (Wm. B. Eerdmans Publishing Co., 1977), pp. 77–88. Used by permission.

55. Gutiérrez, *A Theology of Liberation*, p. 136.

56. Ibid., p. 203.

57. Ibid., p. 136.

58. Ibid., p. 135. Cf. José Miguez-Bonino, "Popular Piety in Latin America," in *The Mystical and Political Dimension of the Christian Faith*, ed. by Claude Geffré and Gustavo

Gutiérrez, Vol. 96 of *Concilium* (Herder & Herder, 1974), pp. 148–157.

59. Mark Twain, *The Adventures of Huckleberry Finn* (New American Library, Signet Classics, 1959), pp. 209–210.

60. Gutiérrez, *A Theology of Liberation,* p. 204.

61. John Macquarrie, *Paths in Spirituality* (Harper & Row, 1972), p. 121.

62. Robert McAfee Brown, *Theology in a New Key: Responding to Liberation Themes* (Westminster Press, 1978), pp. 50–52, 97–100.

63. Johannes B. Metz, "The Future in the Memory of Suffering," in *New Questions on God,* ed. by J. B. Metz, Vol. 76 of *Concilium* (Herder & Herder, 1972), pp. 9–25.

64. Cf. Dorothee Sölle, *Revolutionary Patience,* tr. by Rita and Robert Kimber (Orbis Books, 1977), especially pp. 24–26.

65. Moltmann, *The Church in the Power of the Spirit,* pp. 352–357.

66. Gutiérrez, *A Theology of Liberation,* pp. 204–205.

67. Frederick Herzog, "Liberation Theology Begins at Home," *Christianity and Crisis,* Vol. 34, No. 8 (May 13, 1974), p. 98.

68. See Jürgen Moltmann, *The Experiment Hope,* ed. and tr. by M. Douglas Meeks (Fortress Press, 1975), pp. 30–43.

69. Alan Harrington, *The Immortalist* (Random House, 1969), p. 11.

70. Ibid., pp. 27, 182.

71. Cf. Robert Veatch, *Death, Dying, and the Biological Revolution* (Yale University Press, 1977).

72. Elisabeth Kübler-Ross, *On Death and Dying* (Macmillan Co., 1969), pp. 15–16.

73. Roy Branson, "Is Acceptance a Denial of Death? Another Look at Kübler-Ross," *The Christian Century,* Vol. XCII, No. 17 (May 7, 1975), pp. 464–468.

74. Daniel Callahan, "On Defining a 'Natural Death,' " *Hastings Center Report,* Vol. 7, No. 3 (June 1977), pp. 32–37.

75. Barth, *Church Dogmatics,* Vol. III, Part 2, pp. 638–639.

76. Werner Fuchs, *Todesbilder in der modernen Gesellschaft* (Frankfurt, 1969), p. 228, quoted by Eberhard Jüngel, *Death: The Riddle and the Mystery* (Westminster Press, 1974), p. 133.

77. Raymond Moody, *Life After Life* (Bantam Books, 1976), p. 97.

78. Cf. Langdon Gilkey, *Reaping the Whirlwind: A Christian Interpretation of History* (Seabury Press, 1976), pp. 306–308.

79. Jüngel, *Death: The Riddle and the Mystery,* pp. 77–78.

80. Abraham Heschel, *The Prophets* (Harper & Row, Colophon Books, 1962), pp. 221–278.

81. See Jürgen Moltmann, *The Passion for Life,* tr. by M. Douglas Meeks (Fortress Press, 1978), pp. 19–26.

82. Bonhoeffer, *Letters and Papers from Prison,* p. 157.

83. The preceding paragraph is adapted from my article, "Life Beyond Death," *Theology Today,* Vol. XXXIV, No. 2 (July 1977), p. 187.